"Ruminating over decisions and pr[...] time. In this upbeat and encouragi[...] ers how to escape this mental trap and free up space for life's adventures."

Laura Vanderkam, author of *Off the Clock* and *Juliet's School of Possibilities*

"Any interaction with Anne or her work leaves me feeling calmer about life. She's our wise internet sister who always has solid advice, and this book is no exception."

Kendra Adachi, author of *The Lazy Genius Way*

"With her signature combination of best-friend warmth and expert insight, Anne Bogel has provided a gift in *Don't Overthink It*. For those of us who care about living wisely and contributing well, Anne offers practical, rich perspective on how we can make decisions without getting stuck in 'what-ifs.' *Don't Overthink It* will be a companion for readers as they make transformative decisions and find themselves stumped by everyday dilemmas."

Beth Silvers, coauthor of *I Think You're Wrong (But I'm Listening)* and cohost of the *Pantsuit Politics* podcast

"I've been reading Anne Bogel for over a decade. As I look back, I see that her words have led me to some of the most important insights of my life. Her gift is showing how small shifts—especially in how we think—can open up a new perspective and a new path. While many of us struggle with a world full of choices, both big and small, *Don't Overthink It* does what Anne always does—shows us there's another way."

Sarah Stewart Holland, coauthor of *I Think You're Wrong (But I'm Listening)* and cohost of the *Pantsuit Politics* podcast

"As a card-carrying member of Overthinkers Anonymous, I didn't just want Anne Bogel to write this book, I *needed* her to write it. I am so grateful she did. This isn't just a book about overthinking; it's a practical, doable guide to stop doing it—and to find the wholeness and freedom that come from taking the steps Anne has so thoughtfully provided."

Marybeth Mayhew Whalen, author of nine novels, chronic overthinker, and cofounder of She Reads

"Anne Bogel can read our minds, and our minds are overthinking. She gets it, and she has real answers instead of pithy platitudes. We don't want to live this way—ruminating and caught in negative thought patterns—and Bogel teaches us the way out. With personal tales of wisdom, humor, and truth, *Don't Overthink It* helps us break free. This book will be a permanent fixture on my nightstand."

Patti Callahan Henry, *New York Times* bestselling author of *Becoming Mrs. Lewis*

Don't Overthink It

Don't Overthink It

Make Easier Decisions,
Stop Second-Guessing, and Bring
More Joy to Your Life

Anne Bogel

BakerBooks

a division of Baker Publishing Group
Grand Rapids, Michigan

© 2020 by Anne Bogel

Published by Baker Books
a division of Baker Publishing Group
PO Box 6287, Grand Rapids, MI 49516-6287
www.bakerbooks.com

Printed in the United States of America

Library of Congress Cataloging-in-Publication Data
Names: Bogel, Anne, 1978– author.
Title: Don't overthink it : make easier decisions, stop second-guessing, and bring more joy to your life / Anne Bogel.
Description: Grand Rapids, Michigan : Baker Books, a division of Baker Publishing Group, 2020. |
Identifiers: LCCN 2019033787 | ISBN 9780801094460 (paperback)
Subjects: LCSH: Thought and thinking.
Classification: LCC BF441 .B6255 2020 | DDC 158.1—dc23
LC record available at https://lccn.loc.gov/2019033787

Scripture quotations are from the New Century Version®. Copyright © 2005 by Thomas Nelson. Used by permission. All rights reserved.

This publication is intended to provide helpful and informative material on the subjects addressed. Readers should consult their personal health professionals before adopting any of the suggestions in this book or drawing inferences from it. The author and publisher expressly disclaim responsibility for any adverse effects arising from the use or application of the information contained in this book.

The author is represented by the William K. Jensen Literary Agency.

20   21   22   23   24   25   26   7   6   5   4   3   2

In keeping with biblical principles of creation stewardship, Baker Publishing Group advocates the responsible use of our natural resources. As a member of the Green Press Initiative, our company uses recycled paper when possible. The text paper of this book is composed in part of post-consumer waste.

For
Jackson, Sarah,
Lucy, and Silas.

My mission in life is not merely to survive, but to thrive; and to do so with some passion, some compassion, some humor, and some style.

Maya Angelou

With the new day comes new strength and new thoughts.

Eleanor Roosevelt

Be careful what you think, because your thoughts run your life.

Proverbs 4:23

Contents

Part 3 Let the Sun Shine In

1

How We Spend Our Lives

Far more than you may realize, your experience, your world,
and even your self are the creations of what you focus on.

Winifred Gallagher

I'm scheduled to depart for Nashville in twenty-seven hours, and I can't stop refreshing the forecast. I have a million things to do before I leave—more than I can possibly accomplish—yet I persist in hitting refresh. I can see it's not helping; it's actually making things worse. Yet I keep doing it.

I'm driving south to work on a new project, one I've been planning for months. It wasn't easy to get the date on the calendar, but now it's finally here. My hotel has long been booked and my workbag is freshly packed. I've finalized my itinerary and downloaded a new audiobook for the drive. There's just one wild card: the weather.

All week long, I've been monitoring the volatile storms that threaten to derail my plans. The forecast is not for Southern summer pop-up storms but a massive front coming to blanket the region. My friend first noticed the situation at girls' night earlier this week. While we chatted and drank half-price glasses of wine, she peered over our shoulders at the silenced meteorologist on the bar's TV. "Hey, when do you leave for Nashville?" she asked. "That storm does *not* look good."

Because we've spent dozens of girls' nights discussing our fears, both rational and otherwise, my friends know I'm an uneasy road tripper even on sunny days, and I abhor driving through storms. And they know how, just weeks before, my family had been caught in the worst thunderstorm I'd ever experienced, right on that same stretch of I-65 I would soon be driving again, solo. We were headed to Florida for our annual beach week; my husband, Will, was behind the wheel. Usually I'd be reassured by his steady presence, but this time even he looked fearful. Construction walls meant we couldn't pull over, and the radar showed the rain wouldn't let up for hours. Visibility was practically zero, and I'd told my friends after the fact that it was a miracle we didn't end up in a hundred-car pileup on the interstate.

"Never again," I'd said as I recounted the story.

But the five-day forecast made a repeat performance look possible. Maybe *likely*. "You'd better keep an eye on that forecast," my friend said.

I've taken my friend's words to heart, perhaps too much. This week I've been checking the weather constantly, hoping the storm would dissipate or its path would shift. Neither sunny outcome has materialized.

Instead of fading out, the storm has intensified—along with my anxiety level.

Leaving early isn't an option. I have work to do at home in Louisville. I've also been traveling a lot this season and am not keen on the idea of leaving my family again. I don't want to miss another family dinner or my son's big baseball game on what promises to be a beautiful summer night.

But I don't see how I can drive two hundred miles in the storm.

So now I'm staring at my computer monitor, hoping against hope that my next click will deliver a happier version of reality. But each time, I don't like the new answer The Weather Channel serves up—and so I click again, and again. I make myself walk away from the computer to, you know, *actually accomplish something*, but I can't concentrate with the storm looming. So I sneak back to my screen and check again. I feel more agitated with every click.

Before long, I'm snared in the too-familiar spin cycle of overthinking, unable to focus on anything else. I know the signs: lots of mental action, none of it constructive, all the while knowing I have better things to do. All my mental energy is consumed by the forecast—which I can't do a thing about—instead of the things that actually need my attention.

The more I think about what to do, the less sure I am about the answer. *Should I leave now? Should I wait? Should I keep waiting and hoping?* The deeper I sink into my overthinking spiral, the less confident I feel about my *ability* to decide, and the specific problem in front of me mushrooms into a larger concern: What kind of idiot spends hours staring at The Weather Channel? Shouldn't a competent adult be able to make a simple decision? I'm in danger of losing all perspective, when the humor of it hits me. I text my friend this message:

> Current situation: massively overthinking my trip to Nashville to begin work on a book tentatively titled *Don't Overthink It*.

Overthinking: What It Is, What It Isn't

Anyone who's picked up a book called *Don't Overthink It* can sympathize with me, because you've been there. You know what it feels like to get caught in a loop of unproductive—or even destructive—thought.

When we talk about overthinking, we're not talking about having our basic needs met, like a place to sleep or where we'll find our next meal. Those fundamental questions merit concern and require thought—sometimes lots of it. And we're not talking about major life decisions, like whether to change careers or end a relationship or move across the country. Big decisions like these require dedicated thought. When we talk about overthinking, we're talking about those times when we lavish mental energy on things that don't deserve it. Those times when we can't seem to think about anything else, even though we know our thoughts are better spent elsewhere.

Overthinking takes different forms. Sometimes it looks like worry. We might feel stuck reviewing something we've done in the past or imagining something that might happen in the future. We might spend twenty minutes leaping to imaginative and dire conclusions about that short email from our boss or the note from our child's teacher, or we may construct an elaborate and scary scenario in our mind about why our mom hasn't returned our call. We might lie awake at night wondering what our friends really think of us or if a loved one seems tired of us or if our library fines are getting really and truly out of control.

Sometimes overthinking looks like fretting about the small stuff, devoting disproportionate amounts of brain space to the relatively insignificant. We might catch ourselves in the middle of a long train of thought about whether we should exchange that new pair of jeans for the next size up, or why the washing machine water doesn't seem as hot as it used to and what we should do about it.

Sometimes overthinking looks like second-guessing ourselves. We put just-because flowers on the grocery list, but are they *really* worth the money? We're interested in that concert, but would we be better off with a night in? We want the kids to see the meteor shower, but will the loss of sleep be worth it? Seeing old friends is great, but will we regret using all our vacation time for the reunion? Waffling feels uncomfortable, but without any guiding principles or coherent philosophy, we can't seem to help ourselves.

Whether the concern elbowing into our thoughts is big or small, we recognize the common thread: these thoughts are repetitive, unhealthy, and unhelpful. Our brains are hard at work but accomplishing nothing. It is exhausting and makes us feel crappy. Dr. Susan Nolen-Hoeksema was a psychology professor at Yale whose research focused on women's mental health and well-being. Her studies over a twenty-year period showed that overthinking makes life harder, hurts our relationships, and may contribute to mental disorders like depression, severe anxiety, and alcohol abuse.

Overthinking also carries a significant opportunity cost. Mental energy is not a limitless resource. We have only so much to spend each day, and how we choose to spend it matters. As Annie Dillard writes, "How we spend our days is, of course, how we spend our lives. What we do with this hour, and that one, is what we are doing."

When we spend our time overthinking, *that's what we're doing.*

Let's face it: nobody wants to live a life characterized by overthinking. But it doesn't feel like something we're *choosing*; it feels like something we can't escape. We don't want to fritter away our one precious life second-guessing ourselves about a conversation we had last Thursday or whether we're sick enough to go to the doctor or when we're going to squeeze in a Costco run this week. We want better for ourselves. But we're not sure how to get there.

A friend recently relayed some advice she'd read in a women's magazine that advised to squelch overthinking by resolving not to think about anything that stresses you after dinner. We laughed about this together. It sounds good, but how does one actually *do* it? If one could simply decide not to think about it, we wouldn't have an overthinking problem, would we?

Why is it so hard to untangle this one little thing that looms so large over our lives?

Overthinking Affects Women More Than Men

"We are suffering from an epidemic of overthinking," writes Nolen-Hoeksema. The problem is widespread and, thanks to a combination of neuroscience and socialization, especially plagues women. According to recent studies, women really do have more going on in their brains than men do. In 2017, researchers at the Amen Clinics released imaging data showing "the brains of women in the study were significantly more active in many more areas of the brain than men, especially in the prefrontal cortex, involved with focus and impulse control, and the limbic or emotional areas of the brain, involved with mood and anxiety."

This difference may be a key reason why women are more likely to ruminate, overanalyze, and become paralyzed by indecision. We perseverate instead of act, we worry, we second-guess ourselves. And, whether due to biology or socialization, we focus more on our emotional ties to others than men do. According to Nolen-Hoeksema:

> Women can ruminate about anything and everything—our appearance, our families, our career, our health. We often feel that this is just a part of being a woman.... This may be partly true, but overthinking is also toxic for women. It interferes

with our ability and motivation to solve our problems. It drives some friends and family members away. And it can wreck our emotional health. Women are twice as likely as men to become severely depressed or anxious, and our tendency to overthink appears to be one of the reasons why.

More recent studies indicate that the problem is only becoming worse. One study analyzing birth cohort differences from 1989 to 2016 shows that, despite increased awareness of the dangers, perfectionism is increasing over time. Perfectionism is strongly linked to overthinking, as we'll explore in chapter 3, and the findings that today's young people face more competitive environments and more unrealistic expectations than those of previous generations does not mean good things for their mental or emotional well-being.

It doesn't have to be this way. We can—and must—learn to do better. The consequences are too serious not to.

How to Use This Book

This book is for those of us who, like me, would like to look back one day and declare that our lives were well lived. We can see that living well depends upon thinking well—*about the things that matter*. We want to learn how to overcome decision fatigue, stop feeling overwhelmed, and bring more peace and joy into our lives. That means learning strategies for approaching both our minutes and our days.

Over time, I have deliberately cultivated processes I can trust, ones I turn to when I'm wandering into overthinking territory. Over the years, I've seen how simple strategies and subtle shifts of perspective can trigger lightbulb moments that make some aspect of life easier. These small shifts, taken one at a time, are just that: small. Yet cumulatively, they've transformed my life.

I wanted to share this information with others, and that's why you're holding this book in your hands. Helpful information already exists on this topic, particularly on the subject of rumination, but I couldn't find any existing resources that address all the ways I knew I was overthinking or that share strategies to help me avoid more than just ruminating. As I learned more and more about over-thinking, I grew more and more surprised by just how many facets of our lives overthinking touches. I wanted to write a book that reflected both the far-reaching, destructive effects of overthinking and the not-always-obvious ways we can learn to do better.

I got my start in writing as a blogger. My favorite posts over the years have been those that combine unexpected, seemingly unrelated elements in a way that provides fresh insight by letting the reader see a situation—and herself—in a new way. This book reflects that same approach in subject and scope: it divides things along lines you might not expect, covers topics you may not an-ticipate, and takes a broader view than previous books on the subject. I've done this on purpose, because I believe the subject merits it. And we, as women, need it.

We can learn how to stop overthinking on a persistent basis by doing these things:

- *Setting ourselves up for success.* We'll examine the impor-tance of laying a solid foundation that enables us to become the kind of people who are not prone to overthinking.
- *Taking charge.* We'll learn how to overcome unhealthy thought patterns in the moment and implement practices that make it harder to lapse into these patterns in the first place.
- *Letting the sun shine in.* Overthinkers too often think themselves out of life's simple pleasures, but we'll exam-ine how to smartly think our way *into* them.

You are not doomed to a life of overthinking. You *can* do better, but it won't happen instantly. Getting your thought life under control is a process. It has been for me, as you will see. Some days I do well; I'm satisfied with how I'm spending my hours—and by extension, my life. Sometimes I struggle, and I know I will continue to do so. I'm never going to "arrive," but I can see how far I've come. The process hasn't been easy, but it's been worth it.

And it can be for you too.

In this book, we'll explore the practices that have helped me and so many others overcome overthinking. Some strategies are mundane, while others are easy to grasp and instantly life-changing. Some are about money and memories, while others are about simple abundance. Some are weightier, while others help us reach a decision when the answer isn't obvious.

It's that last strategy that finally jolted me out of my Nashville funk last June. Let's go back to my kitchen table, where I'm locked in to The Weather Channel website, refreshing the page like a madwoman, hoping for a better answer that's never going to come.

My friend replies to my SOS text with laughter and then asks: "What's stressing you out about the travel details?" She asks me to articulate the precise issue, and I do: I tell her I hate my options. Giving voice to that reality doesn't feel like a complaint; it feels like clarity. *I'm not going to be happy either way.*

Even if I don't *like* the outcome, that doesn't mean it's not the *right* outcome. And that frees me to choose.

I'm no longer frantic. I check the forecast—with purpose this time. I check the traffic situation. I push back from the computer with a plan, and I leave a few hours later, twenty-two hours earlier than scheduled. It's not ideal, but it works, and the decision is blessedly behind me.

It only rains a little on the way.

· · · · · · · · · · · · · Next Steps · · · · · · · · · · · · ·

Take the following quiz to see if you are an overthinker.

1. Do you sometimes lavish mental energy on things that don't deserve it?

2. Are there times when you can't seem to think about anything else, even though you know your thoughts are better spent elsewhere?

3. Do you ever feel stuck reviewing something that happened in the past?

4. Do you frequently second-guess yourself?

5. Do you fret about the small stuff and spend too much time thinking about relatively insignificant issues or problems?

6. Do your thoughts sometimes keep you up at night?

7. Do you engage in thoughts you know to be repetitive, unhealthy, and unhelpful?

If you answered yes to some of these questions, you tend to overthink things. Keep reading, because you don't have to keep doing it.

Part 1

Set Yourself Up for Success

2

Work the Process

*Nothing had just happened to her, she had made a choice,
and then she had made another and another after that.
Taken together, the small choices anyone made added up to
a life.*

J. Courtney Sullivan

I have a friend who is, by her own description, a chronic overthinker. She says she was born that way and it's just the way
she is. End of story.

She thinks it's cute, actually—that we women love our families
so much that we can't stop ourselves from worrying about them.
Because we're committed to getting things right—whether in our
homes, our work, or our relationships—it's only natural to think
about them all the time. We just can't help ourselves, bless our
hearts. Whenever her struggle with overthinking comes up in

conversation, she always ends by asking rhetorically, "But what can you do?"

She assumes there's nothing she *can* do. And it's no wonder. When we look around, we see so many women who overthink, who believe these patterns of thought come naturally and there's nothing they can do about them. It's easy to think this is just the way it is.

This misconception is common, but it isn't harmless. Regardless of the facts, my friend's mindset makes change impossible. When we assume we *can't*, it's guaranteed we *won't*. It's true that some of us are naturally more decisive, more laid back, or more confident than others. Some of us *are* more inclined to overthink. But that is the starting point, not the last word. That is where we begin, not where we're destined to end up.

You Have to Believe You Can Change

Overthinking has always come naturally to me. For me, *not* overthinking is *not* effortless. I've had to learn how to get my thought life under control, and even after all these years, I don't expect to *never* overthink. But I'm happy to succeed a significant percentage of the time—so often, in fact, that from the outside it may even appear that *not* overthinking comes naturally to me.

But appearances don't tell the whole story.

This idea was captured by advertisers in a long-running cosmetics campaign built around what is now the most recognizable phrase in 150 years of advertising: "Maybe she's born with it. Maybe it's Maybelline." When I was a kid, I loved these ads. They always showed a beautiful, well-dressed woman, prompting the viewer to wonder if her face looked like that when she woke up or if she relied on Maybelline makeup to get "the look." (Although, even as a kid, it was clear the answer was Maybelline, every time.)

So it goes with overthinking—or, more accurately, *not* over-thinking. Maybe we look at someone who appears to never doubt herself and think, *I wish I could be like that.* Or worse, *I'll never be like that.* She never seems to get pulled into negative thought patterns or to second-guess herself, so why do we? We may assume she was born that way. But what if she wasn't? What if she had to slowly learn, bit by bit?

I admire people who belong in the former camp, but I belong to the latter. It may look effortless now, but trust me—I've had to learn. And so can you. Perfection isn't possible, but change totally is.

Begin to Describe Yourself Differently

In my first book, *Reading People,* I write about how the way we see ourselves has enormous implications for how we live our lives. "I'm the kind of person who _____" is a powerful statement, no matter what goes in that blank. A shift in our sense of identity—that is, a shift in how we fill in that blank—can cause massive changes in our behavior, almost instantly.

Beginning now, I don't want you to describe yourself as a chronic overthinker. Don't call yourself that, not even in your own head. Overthinking is no longer part of your identity, though it may be a behavior you're engaging in right now. Instead, begin to describe yourself—if only in your head—as someone who:

- Is capable of experiencing less decision angst and more joy and peace
- Can learn to make confident, competent decisions
- Doesn't need to habitually second-guess herself
- Is learning how to filter out the unimportant, unhealthy, and unhelpful

- Is developing strategies for stopping overthinking in its tracks
- Is becoming equipped to gracefully pivot when things don't go as planned
- Can put overthinking aside to welcome good things into her life

Shifting your mindset is just the first step, but it's an important one. Now you've got some work to do. Improvement won't happen on its own, and it won't happen overnight, but it *will* happen.

How I Began to Change the Way I See Myself

Two years after I graduated from college, the Twin Towers collapsed. I wasn't close to New York City when it happened; I was on an airplane headed that way from Prague. Hours after departing the Czech Republic, our plane was turned around and sent back to Europe, where, through an unlikely confluence of tragedy and simple bad luck involving 9/11, a bee sting, an allergy, and a German emergency room, I began suffering panic attacks for the first time in my life.

Weeks later, when I finally made it back to the United States, I followed up with my doctor. He told me my experience was common: my elevated stress levels after 9/11 made me susceptible to a full-blown panic attack, triggered by the bee sting. He said we needed to dial down my stress response, and fast, because panic attacks beget more panic attacks. With each one I experienced, I etched grooves in my nervous system that made it that much easier to have another—and another. I didn't want my body to memorize that route.

My doctor prescribed anxiety and blood pressure meds and sent me on my way, but as we said goodbye, he made an offhand comment that changed my life. "The mental arena isn't my area of expertise," he said, "but I know this: your thoughts can be the enemy, or you can make them your ally."

I was intrigued by his observation. I didn't fully grasp what it meant or how to put it into practice, but I understood that my thoughts were intimately connected to my health and well-being—something I'd not previously thought much about—and that exploring this connection was paramount. I set out on an exploratory journey the way avid readers do: I visited the library and bookstore, stockpiling resources on health, meditation, and mindfulness. And I started paying a lot more attention to what I thought about.

As I read, I was surprised to discover how much control I could have over my thought life. The capability had been there all along, but I hadn't realized it. I began to not only understand what it might mean to make my thoughts my ally but also, for the first time, see *how* I could do so.

You Can Learn Strategies to Stop Overthinking

I've had many conversations with women who tell me, "I wish I could stop overthinking," but they don't try to do anything differently. They don't believe it's possible, so they don't attempt to do anything about it. I know what this feels like, because I was one of them. My doctor's offhand comment made me realize that I had the power to change. Once I knew I *could*, I began to explore *how*.

And knowing how changes everything. We won't look for a solution if we don't believe one exists.

Quite recently, my own false assumptions have shut me off from solutions. We have a family minivan, which isn't everyone's dream car, but I like a few things about mine. Topping my list is the camera feature that helps me back up and change lanes safely. I love it, but it used to be fickle. The camera is supposed to display only when I'm in reverse or have my right blinker on, but sometimes it wouldn't turn off when it was supposed to and the display would light up even though I didn't want or need it to. It was incredibly frustrating, but there was nothing to be done about it.

Or so I assumed.

But then last winter, my sixteen-year-old got his learner's permit. At this point, we'd owned the minivan for over a year. One day when our son was behind the wheel, he flipped on the turn signal and felt a button he hadn't noticed before. He asked us, "What does this button do?"

Will and I didn't know about that button; we didn't know what it did. We told him to hit it and see what happened.

Can you guess what the button did? Of course you can. *That button turned off the camera.*

For over a year, my inability to turn off the camera had been frustrating me to no end, but I didn't know the means to turn it off had been right there the whole time. Because I never dreamed there was a solution, I didn't look for one. The answer had been literally at my fingertips, but I didn't know it.

When it comes to overthinking, the same thing is true for many of us. We're bothered by it, but we don't do anything about it because we don't know change is within reach.

Of course, reducing overthinking is not as simple as hitting a button on the turn signal. If only! But we do have strategies at our disposal, and we're going to learn how to use them.

I like to think about wrangling my thought life the same way I think about learning to drive. (It's funny that I keep using car analogies, because I'm not a car person. But the analogy works: the car is a complicated piece of equipment and so is the human brain.) To drive safely, a driver needs to learn basic practices to operate her vehicle: She needs to know how to start the ignition, check her mirrors, use her turn signals, and engage the parking brake. She needs to know how to clean her windshield, put gas in the tank, and change the oil. But that's not all. She also needs to know how to respond to what's happening in front of her—to swerve around a stalled vehicle, brake for a pedestrian, deal with a tailgater, or handle an emergency like a flat tire. These skills keep the car and driver functioning smoothly and enable the driver to respond to trouble when it arises.

The same goes with overthinking. Sometimes we need to defend against an active instance of overthinking in the moment. When we notice we're caught in a negative thought pattern, it's like seeing a stalled vehicle in our lane. We need to change course, and quickly, to avoid unpleasant consequences. In subsequent chapters, we'll learn strategies to overcome active instances of overthinking.

But to stop overthinking on a persistent basis, we want to develop the skills and habits that characterize a helpful thought life, the ones that will keep that vehicle running well for a long time. Getting your thought life under control may feel hard—perhaps so hard it doesn't seem possible. But I invite you to consider that, here at the beginning, it's hard right now.

This Won't Stay Hard Forever

A few years ago, when one of my kids was in tutoring, I was invited to sit in on a session where the tutor ran my child through a challenging numbers exercise. (As in, I had a hard time keeping up.) After my child stumbled through the first column of numbers, the tutor asked if they could try the next harder column together.

My child said, "I think that's too hard." No whining, no complaining—just a simple statement of fact. He thought he couldn't do the work. I wasn't bothered by it.

But the tutor reflexively fired back with, "It's too hard *right now*."

He explained that as my child continued to build his skills, that column wouldn't be hard anymore. They would learn how to do it, together. It's hard today, but it won't stay that way.

Before we left that day, the tutor pulled me aside for a second. He explained how important it is for kids to believe in their core that they can get better and that if they practice, exercises that are nearly impossible today will be possible tomorrow.

"I make my students do hard things," he said, "but those hard things don't stay hard." With practice, those hard things become doable. Soon enough, they'll become second nature.

Learning to think well is a process. Some strategies are simple to implement, while others are harder. Some really will feel like hitting a button, while others will require perseverance. Adopting new mental practices and patterns of thought may feel daunting at first, and it's no wonder. In *The Chemistry of Calm*, Dr. Henry Emmons, an integrative psychiatrist who advocates a holistic approach to mental health problems like depression and anxiety, writes that it's no surprise we feel our current "wild mind" state is our natural way of being. He writes, "Since childhood we have spent many of our waking hours reinforcing our habits of thought. We empower them through attention and repetition. Anything that we practice this consistently we will eventually get good at." We've become good at overthinking, thanks (or no thanks) to all the practice we've put in.

That's why we need to start practicing new strategies—and as we practice new ways of thinking and reinforce new habits of thought, we will become much better at *not* overthinking.

One Small Step at a Time

Getting caught up in overthinking is a vicious cycle. As Emmons explains, "Many of us strengthen unhealthy nerve circuits through repetitive practice. Every time we repeat a fearful or defeatist thought, we strengthen the connections that make it easier to have that thought again." In other words, the more we overthink, the easier it is to keep overthinking.

We have to break the cycle, and we can do that by starting small. Nolen-Hoeksema's research affirms the effectiveness of this strategy. She writes, "Doing something small toward solving our problem often is a foot-in-the-door technique. That small effort makes it easier to get the other foot, and eventually our whole body, in the door. Little victories accumulate until soon we begin to see the end to a problem, and how to get there."

Here's what this can look like in action: a few years ago, a friend was facing a major change in her children's schooling, and she was freaking out about all the options, particularly because this topic had been a huge source of worry in the past. She talked to dozens of parents, checked out stacks of books from the library, and began researching different pedagogical approaches. She quickly became overwhelmed, feeling like she'd need a graduate degree and a fully articulated philosophy of education before she could decide, which would take more time than she had. She lay awake at night running through all the options in her mind, all the possibilities about what could go wrong.

On the verge of a total meltdown, she sought my help because she knew I'd faced a similar choice the year before. I suggested she take it one step at a time. It was okay that she didn't have a fully formed plan right that moment. She could take the next step—a small and doable one—on the path to clarity. And she did. Before the day was over, she had scheduled a school tour and felt much better.

When we're overthinking, the easiest thing to do is keep overthinking. To stop the cycle, we need to interrupt these thought patterns, and we can do that by taking a small step in the right direction. Then it becomes easier to take another right step, and another.

Getting caught up in overthinking may be a vicious cycle, but extracting yourself is a virtuous one. As Emmons says, "If we can stop reinforcing these [negative] patterns by repeated thought, they will gradually weaken. And soon we are able to create new, healthier neural circuits to take the place of the old ones."

As you begin to learn new strategies, my advice—which you'll often see repeated in this book—is to pick a small step and get moving. Pick one thing you can do to begin to disrupt the cycle, even if it's a very small thing. As you move forward, implementing the strategies in this book, trusting the process, you will loosen the hold overthinking has on you. You'll see your confidence and knowledge grow, and as they do, the next steps will become easier.

You are not doomed to a life of overthinking. Trust the process, and get ready for your next step.

············ Next Steps ············

The way we see ourselves has enormous implications for how we live our lives. When it comes to overthinking, how do you currently see yourself? Fill in these blanks:

1. I am the kind of person who

....

....

....

2. How would you like to see yourself in the future?

....

....

....

....

3. I would like to be the kind of person who

....

....

....

....

....

3

Watch What You're Doing

Certainty is missing the point entirely.
Anne Lamott

When my husband was a kid, he faced a recurring dilemma. Whenever his mom went to Target, she invited him to come along, knowing he enjoyed exploring the toy aisle, picking out the family cereal, and maybe buying a pack of baseball cards with his allowance.

Will loved shopping at Target. But not as much as playing with friends in the neighborhood. He wanted to go to Target, but he didn't want to miss the opportunity to play with a friend. Will's greatest fear was that he would return home from an otherwise fun shopping trip to learn a friend had called with an invitation while he'd been out.

Every time his mom invited him to come with her, he had to choose: Should he go to the store or stay home in case a friend became available to play?

His mom would wait, with growing impatience, while he deliberated. He was persistently torn between the two options.

I've heard Will tell his childhood tale of Target angst a hundred times, and it always makes people laugh. It's funny, sure, but also—*we get it*. He was suffering from analysis paralysis, that state in which we overthink things to such a degree that we are completely unable to decide. We've all been there—and not just when we were kids. Let's be honest, we grown-ups have way more experience overthinking than your typical seven-year-old.

While it's easy to see Will's behavior for what it was, analysis paralysis isn't always so easy to recognize in our own lives. We lack the perspective to see our own behavior clearly; we're too close, too caught up in it, to recognize when our own thought patterns become problematic. We may see our behavior as completely rational and fail to realize that the decision-making styles we rely on—and assume are more or less serving us well—are, in fact, incredibly hospitable to overthinking.

In order to change our overthinking ways, we have to notice the ways we're overthinking. We need to watch what we're doing, observing our own behavior with a measure of the same objectivity we have for Will's childhood self.

Spotting the Signs of Analysis Paralysis

Analysis paralysis is one of the most common manifestations of overthinking. When we're in its grip, the problem is not the underlying decision itself but the way we approach it. Instead of helping us solve the problem, our mental habits make us more entrenched in indecision.

Analysis paralysis is dangerous because, left alone, it will never resolve itself. We can't *think* our way out of it. Unless we recognize what's happening and intervene, we will remain stuck.

Common signs of analysis paralysis include:

- Repeatedly putting off decisions until later
- Postponing a decision in hopes that a better option will present itself
- Seeking more options when we already have enough
- Constantly reviewing the same information we've already gathered
- Fearing we will make the wrong decision
- Waiting so long to decide that we miss the opportunity to do so
- Second-guessing a decision after it is made

Why We Overthink: Causes of Analysis Paralysis

Analysis paralysis does not affect us all equally; some of us are more inclined than others to get caught in this specific trap. Sometimes our less helpful tendencies, like perfectionism, predictably reel us in. Sometimes we're snared by more insidious means when our best qualities, like intelligence and curiosity, get us into trouble.

When approaching a decision, we may get stuck for a variety of reasons. For example, we may enjoy exploring the options or feel uncertain about what to do, or we may be driven by a perfectionistic belief that the right answer is out there somewhere, waiting to be found.

Intellectual Curiosity

When faced with a decision, intellectually curious people habitually seek more information about the matter at hand. They're eager to learn more for the sake of learning and find the pursuit of new knowledge inherently interesting. When seeking a solution, highly intelligent people may see whole landscapes of possibilities that others don't see—which may inadvertently lead them to make simple decisions needlessly complex.

These positive traits have an unintended consequence: they make us prone to analysis paralysis because they prod us to search for additional options, whether or not we need them. Those extra options don't lead to better decisions; they just overwhelm us. And when we're overwhelmed, we can't decide *anything*.

Intelligence and curiosity don't inevitably cause analysis paralysis, thank goodness. But if we're unaware of the connection, these positive qualities are more likely to lead us astray.

Information Overload

When we're making a decision, more information can be a good thing. The problem is not the impulse to gather information but the degree to which we follow it. Gathering data and examining options are beneficial—but at a certain point, that hunt for information not only has diminishing returns but becomes actively unhelpful. (Information is good until it's bad. See how sneaky overthinking is?) Before long, we're trapped by our own thoughts, believing that if only we can find a new data point, identify the needed resource, or think a little harder about the issue, the answer will become clear.

Instead, that extra information only further overwhelms us. When we hold out for more data points, we're not being smart; we're sabotaging ourselves. We're not moving toward a solution; instead, we're actively making our situation worse.

Once established, the cycle is difficult to break. When—or *if*—we do ultimately reach a decision, we're less sure about the outcome than we were before. Imagine my poor husband debating whether to go to Target. Because he'd overthought the situation, no matter what he chose, he wasn't going to be happy. The same is true for us when we face our own decisions. Because of our overanalysis, we'll be less satisfied with the outcome, even if we arrive at an objectively better one.

If we aren't aware that analysis paralysis is the cause of our troubles, the cycle continues. Our dissatisfaction spurs us to analyze even more the next time we face a decision, which leads to greater paralysis.

Perfectionism

Years ago, my husband and I needed to tile the bathroom in our first house. We couldn't find a contractor to do it at a price we could afford, so we resolved to do it ourselves.

During the project, I kept running to Home Depot for supplies, and every time I entered the tile department, I'd see a big sign hanging from the rafters that urged shoppers to "Do it right or do it again." Each time I saw it, I thought two things: *Yes, exactly!* and *I sure hope I'm doing it right, because I don't want to do it again.*

Back then I made a critical error, assuming that *right* meant the same thing as *perfect.* It's one thing to value high standards, but there's a difference between high standards and perfection. I hope Home Depot has retired that stupid slogan by now, because it haunted me for years, bringing my submerged inner perfectionist roaring back whenever I thought about it.

Like many, I'm well acquainted with perfectionism. When I was younger, I didn't perceive the ways perfectionism had infiltrated my thought life, nor did I perceive its ripple effects—indecision, irritability, analysis paralysis. I wasn't able to name perfectionism as a struggle, which meant it had a big advantage in our ongoing tug-of-war.

When we don't realize perfectionism has a hold on us, it can exert an unsettling degree of control over our behavior. Calling perfectionism what it is deprives it of its power.

Perfectionism may manifest as any of the following:

- Regular procrastination
- A need to find the "right" answer before moving forward
- All-or-nothing thinking
- Struggles with completing a project because there's always more we could do
- A critical eye that homes in on imperfections
- Replaying what we wished we'd said in our mind following a conversation
- Frequently second-guessing past decisions

Many are shocked to discover that perfectionism and overthinking go hand in hand; it's a villain we recognize, in a role we don't expect. But once we understand the connection, we can see how perfectionistic tendencies fuel overthinking. When we face a decision, the impossibly high standards demanded by perfectionism are just that—impossible. Whether we're analyzing an imminent decision to death or we're stuck in the past, regretting what we chose, we always want to get the decision right. But if we equate right with perfect, it is deadly—because when we aim for perfection, we freeze. When perfectionism reigns, if we can't tell what the absolute, unquestionable best option is in a given situation, we do nothing—except fret about it. *Hello, analysis paralysis.*

The perils of overthinking before we make a decision are obvious: we end up like seven-year-old Will, unable to stay and unable to go. But overthinking isn't confined to happening before our decisions. Perfectionism-driven overthinking often dwells in the space of what-ifs and second-guessing. The moment of decision may have passed, but we can still remain fixated on the decision, analyzing what we *should* have done.

How many of us have tortured ourselves with visions of what we wish we had said or done in the moment? Even if we handled the situation well, we may focus on the one thing we wish we'd done differently. Though the decision has long been made, we can't put it behind us. Instead of weighing our options, making a decision, and moving on, we keep going back to the beginning of the decision-making process, wondering if we made the right choice and if it's too late to make a different one.

All this second-guessing takes a tremendous amount of time and energy, adds considerably to our stress loads, and limits our capacity to make wise decisions in the future.

Antidotes to Analysis Paralysis

Obviously, if it were easy to stop overthinking, we all would have stopped a long time ago. We need actionable strategies to help us overcome analysis paralysis.

Do a Reality Check

We get in trouble when we act as though the ideal answers to our questions are out there somewhere. We may believe that when we finally discover the right answer, it will seem obvious. But the right answer is rarely out there somewhere—and so we stew and stew, without arriving at a resolution, our overthinking manifesting as worry, doubt, and stagnation.

We can't keep searching for perfect solutions, interesting as the pursuit may be, because perfect solutions don't exist. There's seldom one right answer; in reality, there are more often many good answers.

Get Moving

To extricate yourself from analysis paralysis, you don't need more information. You need to *act*.

I don't necessarily mean something big and bold—although that's certainly called for at times. Even taking a baby step forward can shift your momentum and get you unstuck. Your options are numerous, and we'll cover more of them in this book: take a small step, set a deadline, make a list, or consult a friend (their objectivity will help you get out of your own head). Maybe you need to just pick something or get someone else to do it for you.

"Yes," you say, "but if I'm paralyzed, how do I act?" That's a good question. You may need to change your frame of mind.

Kick Perfectionism to the Curb

When we were painting my living room, my dad helped me see how instead of inspiring us to do good work, perfectionism makes us unhappy and prevents us from appreciating the good things in front of us. I was actively trying to paint a razor-straight green line right where the wall met the white ceiling. My line was a bit shaky, and I commented that the paint job wasn't turning out the way I'd hoped. He laughed and said that's the problem with painting your own house—you're not as happy with the result as you would be if you weren't the one doing the painting. "If someone else did the hard work, you'd think it looked great," he said. "But when you're the painter, you're acutely aware of every single place you goofed. You can do a good job and still feel like you messed it up."

He was right. I *had* done a good job. But as long as I insisted on comparing my good outcome to the ideal one in my head, I was going to make myself miserable. Perfectionism makes us critical, uptight, and generally not fun to be around. Plus, we're more likely to overthink when we're in a bad mood. There's no need to be so hard on ourselves, because it doesn't have to be perfect to be good.

Give Yourself Permission to Fail

It's one thing to *want* to loosen the hold perfectionism has on you, but how do you actually *do* it? The remedy is to give yourself permission to fail—failure being defined as "anything short of absolute perfection"—and grace when you actually do.

Like it or not, failure can be incredibly instructive. Ironically, sometimes we get better results when we screw up than if we never get it wrong. If mistakes aren't okay, we miss out on one of the fastest, most effective ways to learn. But *failure* can be a scary word to throw around, especially for recovering perfectionists like me. To learn from it, we need to get comfortable with it—and a change in terminology can help. I've learned to say, "Let's experiment," because that phrase doesn't make my insides clench up like the word *failure* does. An experiment is neutral, dispassionate. There's none of that paralyzing pressure to get it right. When I try an experiment, success is getting an outcome. *Any* outcome. The goal is to get results, not a win.

Adopt a "Try It and See What Happens" Approach

Lest you think embracing failure is a feel-good technique for softies, know that there are compelling reasons to adopt a "try it and see what happens" approach. It's not weak or lazy, it's savvy. My husband used to work in software development, where "minimum viable product" is a phrase they toss around a lot. Software developers take an iterative approach to product development—they never try to deliver a perfect product on the first attempt. Instead, they want to build an imperfect product, and they want to do it quickly. When they have something to work with, they can quickly see what works and what doesn't, give it to users to test, and identify core problems and possible solutions—not in the abstract, but in a real, tangible way. Creating an imperfect product helps developers determine if pursuing a perfect version is even worth it. Not everything is worth doing perfectly.

With an experiment, there's no "do it right or do it again." Instead, it's "do it and see what happens." Or "do it and *then* do it again," incorporating whatever you learned the first time. This iterative approach frees us from the need to always get it right. Instead of waiting to feel certain before we take action, we can get good information, and fast, by trying something and seeing what happens next. There's no agonizing over the right decision, and there are rarely regrets. Because all you need is an answer, not a victory.

As we move forward, I'm going to invite you to experiment with the strategies in this book—with no agonizing and no regrets. Identify which ones seem most promising to you, give them a try, and see what happens next.

Putting It All Together

Let me show you what working this process might look like in real life with an ordinary, low-stakes example of recognizing and overcoming analysis paralysis. As I write this, I feel like I'm devoting an awful lot of ink to an inconsequential decision. But since this is exactly what happens when overthinking hijacks our thought processes, I'm going for it.

For well over a decade, my family of six has spent one week each summer at a certain Gulf Coast beach. We love our beach week but have never loved getting there. The drive takes about eleven hours, and that's a long time to spend cooped up in a minivan. We used to always make the drive in one long day, assuming it would be best to power through and get it over with.

But Will and I long wondered if we would be less miserable if we broke the trip into two segments. For reasons I cannot explain, my kids adore hotel pools and the kind of all-you-can-eat breakfast served at your typical Holiday Inn Express. What if we drove halfway, spent the night at a hotel, and drove the rest of the way in the morning?

We debated doing this for years—literal years, maybe six or seven. Every summer as our departure date approached, we'd revisit the question yet again, consider all the options, resist making up our minds, and finally wait so long to decide that the opportunity passed us by. We weren't certain trying a new way was the right thing, so we didn't act.

But a few years ago, I discovered the power of the iterative approach and began working on my experimental mindset. That year, when decision time rolled around, we didn't endlessly debate, nor did we once again make pros and cons lists, because we'd already thought about the issue plenty. I'd been overthinking this issue for years without realizing that's what I was doing. This time I recognized the overthinking for what it was. And I knew what to do.

First, I did a reality check. There wasn't one perfect answer to our driving dilemma. Either option got us to the beach.

Then I got moving. I quizzed a friend who always breaks long drives into multiple days about her experience, and then I made sure hotels were available for the night we needed.

Next, I explicitly gave myself permission to fail. I hadn't wanted to act because I'd been afraid we wouldn't like the new way—and it's hard to act when you're afraid of getting it wrong. When I could perceive it was unjustified fear holding me back, I felt free to move forward.

And finally, since we'd been thinking about this for ages, we decided to try it and see what happened. We'd consider it an experiment. If we preferred the new way, great. But if we tried it and didn't like it, at least we'd stop wondering if another way might be better. We didn't have to prefer the new way to the old to consider this little experiment a success.

In the end, we all preferred our two-day drive to the beach with the hotel stopover. But if it hadn't gone well—if we swore we never wanted to do it again—it wouldn't have been a mistake, because the goal was to get a result, not the best possible experience. No need to second-guess our decision for years to come.

What's Happening in Your Life?

When we don't recognize our overthinking behavior for what it is, it's impossible to get over it. And as long as we rely on decision-making styles that encourage overthinking, we're going to spend a lot of time overthinking. But once we see what's really going on, we can begin to change. It will feel like a battle at first—especially if we've been analyzing things to death our whole lives—but with time, it will feel like a habit.

·············· Next Steps ··············

With fresh eyes, take a look at your own behavior.

1. Where are you experiencing analysis paralysis right
   now?

   ....

   ....

   ....

2. Where are you experiencing perfectionism?

   ....

   ....

   ....

   ....

3. What factors are keeping you stuck?

   ....

   ....

   ....

   ....

   ....

4. What mini-experiments can you implement in order to move forward?

....

....

....

....

....

4

Decide What Matters

"Would you tell me, please, which way I ought to go from here?"
"That depends a good deal on where you want to get to," said the Cat.

Lewis Carroll

I hate to fly. Whenever I'm presented with the opportunity to take a trip, big or small, that requires an airplane, I usually torture myself by debating about whether to go. I hardly ever give a quick yes, even if it's something I—or at least part of me—really want to do. The utter discomfort of plane travel always makes me withhold my yes.

So I was surprised by my friend Ally's own trip. The last time I saw Ally, she was suffering from brutal jet lag because she'd just returned from a quick trip to Thailand. She'd traveled thirty hours and flown literally halfway around the world to spend just four days on the ground. I'm always curious about what compels people to take those thirteen-hour flights. I'm not sure I could do it myself, so whatever awaits them on the other end must be *really* worth it.

At the time, Will and I were debating whether to take a long trip of our own. Long for us, that is. We were considering a December trip to Scotland, and though our longest flight would "only" be nine hours, that was still far too long by my standards. By the time I saw Ally, we'd already been waffling for a while. I wanted to go, but I did not want to get on that plane, and that had kept me from saying yes. I knew I was overthinking it, because instead of working on solving the problem, I was obsessing about the unpleasantness of the flight and the inconvenience of the timing. The flight didn't make it an automatic no, but I needed a compelling reason to get on that plane. I didn't know how to approach the decision. How could I know if this trip was worth taking?

But here Ally had gone off to Thailand. She already traveled regularly for work and wasn't eager to leave town any more than she had to. And she had still said yes to a demanding trip halfway around the world. Why?

With my own looming travel decisions firmly in mind, I told Ally how much I hated to fly and that I was impressed by what her own trip had demanded of her. "Was it tough to decide?" I asked, expecting the answer to be an emphatic yes.

"Not at all," she said. "When I found out about the trip, I didn't have to think about it. I didn't even wait to hear the details. I just said, 'Yes! Let's go.'"

How was this possible? I couldn't believe it, yet I knew Ally wouldn't make such a decision lightly. She's not impulsive by nature, so I was struck by her decisiveness, which couldn't have been more different from my ongoing deliberations about international travel. How on earth did she do it?

Our Values Can Drive Our Decisions

Ally said the choice was easy because *she didn't have to think about it*. Long ago, she made a single decision that continues to influence her ongoing decisions, both big and small, and her Thailand trip was one of them.

Ally explained that her decisions today flowed naturally out of her core values—values she had decided would guide her future decision-making. She told me she'd been in an abusive marriage for a few years, but thanks to help from strong friendships and support networks, she was able to find her way out. Because of her past, today Ally springs into action for abused women as a way to give back what was given to her. Anytime she has an opportunity to serve women who have been exploited, neglected, or abused in any way, she responds by opening her checkbook, participating in the fund-raising event, meeting with a stranger to chat, even saying yes to the trip halfway around the world. Whenever she's invited to support, equip, and empower women who have been exploited, abused, or manipulated, Ally says yes— even if she needs to rearrange work and travel schedules or the cost is substantial.

Because Ally has this big-picture value firmly in place and consciously relies on it when making decisions, she doesn't agonize about how to spend her time, money, and energy. When a choice that involves women who have been exploited, neglected, or abused presents itself, she barely has to think about what to do. In the same way, when we have a broader vision for our lives, many of the decisions we face become simple, because we have a reliable framework for making them. Because we made a single decision—that is, deciding on a big-picture value—we can see all other decisions as parts of a whole instead of as an endless string of isolated decisions. When a decision touches on our values, we have little to think about. With our internal world in order, we can move outward in the right direction. These values can guide our lives in the big pieces and the day-to-day stuff. Whether we're going to Thailand or the grocery store, *what we do* can flow naturally out of *who we are.*

How Our Values Impact Our Decision-Making

We all face numerous decisions every day. Some are significant, like flying across oceans. Some are quotidian, like choosing what's for dinner. Some are unavoidable, some we invite into our lives. But all these decisions demand our attention. We can streamline them, harnessing this values-driven approach to decision-making by identifying what matters to us. Our values can guide decisions big and small, short-term and long-term.

Our Values Can Clarify Our Objectives

When I began questioning people whose decision-making process I admired, people whom I knew not to be overthinkers, it was uncanny how often they used the same word: *values* or *values-driven.* They echoed Ally, saying they try to make decisions based on who they are and what they care about. Naming these values clarifies their objectives and keeps them out of the weeds of day-in and day-out decisions.

Here's an example of what it can look like to stay out of the weeds. Earlier this year, Will and I were in the fortunate position of needing to choose between two good schooling options for one of our kids, and we were struggling. How could we know which one would suit us best? I asked my friend, a retired schoolteacher, for her thoughts.

"I can't tell you what you should do," she said, "but I know how I would decide." When she's debating between options, she always gives preference to the one closer to home, because she wants her life to be rooted in her neighborhood as much as possible. She wants to actually know her neighbors, and she doesn't want to spend her life in the car. So when she's deciding between multiple options, she chooses the option closest to home unless there is a persuasive reason not to. This holds true for big decisions, like choosing which school to attend, and smaller ones, like where to buy groceries or get her hair cut or find a book club. She wants to live her life in actual physical community, and she welcomes the opportunity to bump into her neighbors at carpool or her fellow book club members at the grocery store.

I nodded as my friend described her big-picture value of community, recognizing that Will and I valued this same thing. In fact, we'd moved to our current home a few years ago *because* the new location aligned more clearly with our values: we were seeking a neighborhood that was more walkable, closer to the places we already spent our time, and more diverse, both racially and socioeconomically.

As my friend described her family's schooling choices, I realized our common value of community could guide my own family's schooling decisions as well—and our excruciating choice suddenly became a lot easier. And so this year, my son transferred to a new school just a few blocks from our home. Now we walk to school and see school families in the neighborhood and bump into them at the library. This choice has felt right for who we are as a family, because it reflects what we care about.

Our Values Can Influence How We Spend Our Time and Money

When we harness a values-driven decision-making process, we can proactively allocate our resources for the things that matter most to us. In my own family, Will and I value showing up. It hasn't always been this way. This is a value we first had to discover and then begin to consciously rely on when making decisions.

We started hesitantly living out this value years ago when we were invited to visit college friends we hadn't seen in a while. We *said* we believe people are a good use of our time, money, and energy, and there's no substitute for being there in person. And so to consistently live out this value, we knew we should go—even though the trip was poorly timed, and several of our children still needed diapers, naps, and early bedtimes. A friend once put it like this: "If you care, you'll be there. If you don't, you won't." This little rhyme is not an inviolable rule but a rule of thumb, and it's sprung to mind when we've had to make difficult choices in the intervening years.

Naming "showing up" a big-picture value has made those choices much easier, and we've grown accustomed to making decisions this way. We travel to be at weddings without endlessly debating if the trip is "worth it." We recently bought pricey plane tickets for an inconvenient family reunion, because there's nothing like being there. When friends invited us to join them in celebrating a big family milestone hundreds of miles away, it took just a few minutes to decide. We *could* make the trip happen, so we *did*. We sometimes meet up with old friends in faraway places, not for a wedding or graduation, but just because everyone's getting together. This value applies to my work as well. I prioritize visits with writer friends and colleagues, both in town and across the country, because I've never regretted making the effort to see people in person.

We don't show up only for life's big moments, but having experienced the significance of showing up, we try to be there for the small ones as well. When people we love are celebrating, we try to be there, in person, to celebrate with them. When people we love are hurting, we try to be there for them, even if we can't "fix" anything. *If you care, you'll be there.*

We don't live out this value perfectly, because no matter how much we care, we can't always be there. Sometimes it's prohibitively expensive or logistically impossible, like when two friends got married in different cities the same weekend. But we do the best we can—and more often than not, we rearrange our schedules so we can see the people who matter to us. When it comes to showing up, we err on the side of being there.

Our Values Can Shape Where We Focus Our Attention and Energy

Our values can also influence what we choose to keep before our minds—what we think about, which books we choose to read, what kind of news we pay attention to, which issues we commit to caring about. For example, if you value being an informed citizen on the national and local levels, then we should see the evidence of it in your life. You could read community newsletters to keep up-to-date on local events, chat with your neighbors about local happenings, or subscribe to a newspaper you've come to trust and read it on a regular schedule. All these are ways to live out this value.

I've found it's easier to live out my values when I keep them at the forefront of my attention, and one of my favorite ways to do this is by reading nonfiction. To keep my focus where I want it, I read about things that matter to me. This works because the clearer I am on my values, the easier it is for what I do to flow naturally out of who I am. I value being a present, compassionate parent, and when I'm reading a good book about relationships, like Brené Brown's *Daring Greatly*, I'm attuned to the dynamics of my own. I value working hard on my craft, and when I'm reading a good writing book, like John McPhee's *Draft No. 4*, I'm inspired to put my butt in my chair and write, even when I don't feel like it. I value taking good care of my body, and when

I'm reading about nutrition and exercise, I'm inspired to eat well and get moving.

Fact-Checking Our Values

Our lives should reflect who we are and what we care about. We may think we know what we value but find that those values don't actually influence our decisions. This inconsistency makes it impossible for our decisions to flow naturally. We may say we value family, but we're never home for dinner. We may say we care about charity work, but give it none of our time, money, or attention. I talk to plenty of people who say they believe reading is important and don't have anything preventing them from doing so, but they don't actually read. We may *say* one thing, but if we actually *do* another, then we don't really value what we say we do.

To ensure our values align with our actual lives, we need to "fact-check" ourselves by asking, "What does my behavior indicate I value?" If you're uncertain, recruit a friend to help you see your behavior with fresh eyes. If you don't like what you see, it's time to do some tweaking.

Case in point. My uncle used to smoke regularly. He considered himself a healthy person, except for this one habit. He thought about quitting for years. He was a physician, and his patients constantly gave him a hard time about being a smoker. He knew he should quit, of course, but he never took action. "Maybe one day," he told himself.

Then "one day" arrived in a mundane way. He was running late, took the elevator to his floor, rushed down the hall to his office, and greeted his nurse.

"Good morning," she said. "I was so relieved to hear you coming."

Puzzled, he asked, "How did you know it was me?"

Now *she* was puzzled; she'd thought the answer was obvious. "We always know when you get off the elevator," she explained. "We can hear your cough all the way down the hall."

My uncle had always thought of himself as a healthy person and was stunned to realize that his own staff perceived him to be unhealthy. This realization brought instant clarity, and he knew one of those pictures had to change. After years of thinking about it, he quit cold turkey. I've heard quitting smoking is tough, but my uncle's journey was made much easier by one key thing: he wanted to be a person who lived a healthy lifestyle. Once his eyes were opened, he couldn't remain a smoker, because smoking conflicted with that value.

Like my uncle (accidentally) did, you can purposefully check your behavior against your actual life to see if you're in alignment. When I'm wondering if my life and my values are in sync, I've found it helpful to take a look at my calendar, because it reflects those things I value enough to actually plan for.

Will took this a step further. He decided he wanted to support arts events in the community, so he added a dedicated arts calendar to our family's Google calendar. Things like book signings, concerts, and library events are color-coded purple on our calendar so we can see at a glance if we're actually showing up for the arts. Now when we're considering whether we want to attend a free author talk at the bookstore or a concert in the park, we don't view it as a onetime choice about how to spend a Tuesday night. Instead, we make the decision in light of our values.

Just last week, our arts calendar showed that we'd long planned to attend the grand reopening of a local library branch that means a lot to my family—the "library next door" I write about in *I'd Rather Be Reading*. The ribbon-cutting ceremony fell in the middle of a busy workday, in the middle of a season that was jam-packed both personally and professionally. Will and I *really* didn't want to take the time to go. For sixty seconds that morning, we debated skipping it to get some work done. Would anyone really miss us? But we value supporting the arts in our community, and the libraries in particular. This specific branch and the people who work there mean a lot to us, and we value showing up for people and causes we care about. At the time, the library system in our town was facing another round of budget cuts, and our presence at this event—our physical show of support—mattered. To keep our values and actions in alignment, it was clear we had to go.

What Matters to You?

What do you value? What kind of person do you want to be? What big-picture values matter most to you? You may be able to rattle off a few instantly, and that's great. I hope this chapter gives you ideas for spotting how you're currently living those out and how you can bring your values and decisions into better alignment.

If you're frustrated that your big-picture values are unclear, take heart. It's okay if you don't have a completely coherent big picture. You can live your way into it; that's part of the discovery process. Once Ally articulated her values, she didn't immediately jump on a plane to Thailand; she got active in her community. Before I flew across the country for a family reunion, I showed up to coffee down the street with a friend. If we're not used to relying on our values to drive our decisions, we may feel hesitant at first, and that's okay. With practice, it will become second nature.

If you are struggling to identify your values, a twofold approach may be helpful. First, you can examine whether unarticulated values are already influencing your decision-making process. To spot these, pay attention to where you spend your time, money, energy, and attention, because we tend to allocate our resources to the things that matter to us. When you do this, do your values begin to emerge? If yes—and you like what you see—you can begin to consciously live those out more thoroughly.

Second, if you don't like the values that emerge, you can identify new values. Some commonly identified core values are authenticity, honesty, kindness, reliability, and loyalty. When I asked friends to identify core values they felt were less common, they named things like lifelong learning, friendship, weirdness, humor, a spirit of adventure, sleeping well at night, a commitment to trying new things, and a healthy lifestyle. Your values don't need to be right for everyone, but they do need to be right for you.

When choosing and discovering new values, thinking about who you are as a person and what kind of person you want to be can bring clarity. How do you want to spend your time? What causes do you care about? When have you felt happy or proud or fulfilled? What was happening then, and why were those experiences so meaningful? The answer may not be clear at first, but a hunch is all you need to move forward. Remember, you're going to live your way into it. You can still move forward down the path even if you don't yet know exactly where that path will lead. Keep moving, and keep paying attention.

With thoughtfulness and practice, all of us can develop consistent filters for making decisions. It may not be easy, but it's simple, because it starts with us—with who we are and what we care about.

Identifying the Value Helps You Decide

Nowadays when I feel stuck making a decision, I ask myself, *Do I hold a value that can inform this decision?* When the answer is yes—and it often is—the decision becomes a whole lot easier.

That was the case with our Scotland deliberations. I'd been overthinking the trip for months, but when Ally unknowingly prompted me to look at it through the lens of my values, I could finally see a convincing reason to get on that airplane. Several reasons, actually. Will and I value experiencing new things together. We value showing up for people we care about, and we'd get to spend time with friends in Scotland. We value new literary experiences, and we'd been invited to take part in an epic one in Scotland's national book town. We value not going into debt, and we had enough points to cover the international airfare, by far the most expensive part of the trip, and savings earmarked for travel to cover the rest.

So far, so good—but that didn't make the long flight any more palatable. That's when I remembered what a mentor once told me: decisions made out of fear are not good decisions. I knew she was right. Staying home because I was afraid of the flight would have been disappointing for everyone and inconsistent with who I am and who I want to be.

We stopped overthinking and decided to take the trip. How could we not? Our values overwhelmingly indicated that, for us, this choice made a whole lot of sense.

··········· Next Steps ·············

1. What do you value?

   ....

   ....

   ....

   ....

2. What kind of person do you want to be?

   ....

   ....

   ....

   ....

3. What big-picture values matter most to you?

   ....

   ....

   ....

   ....

4. How do you want to spend your time?

....

....

....

....

....

5. What causes do you care about?

....

....

....

....

....

6. When have you felt happy, proud, or fulfilled? Why were those experiences so meaningful?

....

....

....

....

....

7. Where do you currently spend your time, money, energy, and attention?

....

....

....

....

8. Are there any new values you'd like to identify for yourself? If so, what are they?

....

....

....

....

5

Take Time to Make Time

*Being a responsible adult is the most underrated form of
self-care. Yes I mean: live within your means, make dentist
appointments, save money, plan meals, wash your face before
bed, go for walks, cook for people, keep your house clean, go
to bed at a decent hour, all that boring stuff. Routines make
everything in your life better and this is absolutely the most
overlooked and underestimated form of self-care.*

Sarah Bessey

School was starting in three days, so it was time to finally
cross the last back-to-school task off the list. A widespread
hepatitis outbreak had just triggered a change in our state's immunization requirements, and a previously optional vaccination
was now mandatory. Like many schoolchildren, my kids had
already had the shot, but if they wanted to attend school the first
day, they needed the paperwork to prove it.

I'd been determined not to leave this undone till the last minute, so I'd gathered the necessary papers from our pediatrician at our regularly scheduled checkups way back in July. Those immunization certificates were hard won: the appointment had taken forever, three times as long as any doctor's appointment should, and I walked out clutching them like a prize.

I considered scanning the forms immediately and sending them right to the kids' schools, but that day was jam-packed with appointments all over the city, as was the next, and after that we were leaving town. Thankfully, the schools didn't need them for weeks. The paperwork could wait.

Or so I thought.

We left for our trip, and I forgot about the papers. When I remembered weeks later, I couldn't find them anywhere. I assumed Will had done something with them—maybe even sent them to the schools—and made a note to ask him about it. But I kept postponing the task till the next day and the next—until right before school started, just as we were going to bed, I remembered to ask Will about the papers. He said he didn't know where they were. Suddenly, I was worried—and now that this loose end was dangling in front of me, I feared I wouldn't be able to sleep until I tied it.

And I couldn't. Though it was already well past my bedtime, I combed the house in search of the certificates, checking every place I could think of, over and over again. They were nowhere to be found.

As I pinged from room to room, I started mentally outlining what I would do if I couldn't find the papers. Would I have to go back to the pediatrician? They needed three business days' notice for paperwork, and you had to show up in person. I began to calculate how many hours of my life it would take to get replacements, if it came to that: one hour at the office, twenty minutes in the car each way. Was it even possible to get replacements before the first day of school? What would happen if my kids couldn't start on time? I was quickly spiraling from "my paperwork is a mess right now" to "my whole life is a mess."

While I perceived I was spinning my wheels, wasting energy and getting all upset for nothing—I was writing this book at the time, after all—I couldn't pull myself out of the cycle. Or chose not to. But then again, it's hard to *choose* anything when it's past your bedtime and you've whipped yourself into a frenzy.

If I hadn't already known I was overthinking, my outward behavior would have given it away. It was almost like I was acting out the detrimental cycle of thought that ensnared me. I literally roved in circles through my house, looking in the same places for those papers, growing more agitated each time I did. My thoughts *and* actions were repetitive, unhealthy, and unhelpful. I felt exhausted, even though I hadn't accomplished anything.

Our Habits Can Serve Us—or Not

We tend to think of overthinking as something that happens in our heads. But overthinking is systemic. We also see its causes and evidence on our to-do lists, in our laundry piles, and in our habits—both mental and physical. It's about not only what we *think* but also what we *do*. My paperwork problem didn't begin when I realized the papers were missing; it began when I put off doing something that needed to be done. I didn't just delay the task, I made it way more complicated—and that means I needed heaps more brain power to finally get it done.

Our habits can serve us or they can be our undoing. My habits were undoing me.

It's both discouraging and empowering to realize how many problems we create for ourselves when we neglect the basic tenets of responsible adulthood. It's discouraging because even if we don't want to, we need to do these things. Many of these tasks—basic, boring things like keeping your desk tidy enough to find what you're looking for, getting enough sleep so your brain can function properly, and scanning those papers for the school secretary—don't feel important in the moment. They may feel more like time-*wasters* than sanity-*makers* at the time, but they give us an incredible payback on our small effort. It's empowering because these habits are well within our control. For better or worse, these basics are essential, and setting up systems to ensure they actually get done has a profound effect on our mental load. When we establish the right habits—in our physical spaces, with our physical bodies—we can stop much overthinking before it starts, because the things that need to get done actually get done. We'll never waste an hour frantically searching the house for something we should have taken care of long ago.

We may not realize the importance of these habits until they fail us. A usually organized friend lost her credit card for a week last summer and finally found it in her wallet because she hadn't taken the extra three seconds at the checkout to return it to its usual slot. When you spend your time searching for your credit card, that is what you are doing with your life. Wouldn't you rather be doing more interesting things?

Completing the Cycle

Just yesterday I spent half an hour looking for a paperback I needed for a book club discussion. Around here, we keep books all over the house—in my office, the library, the kids' rooms, the basement—and we like it that way. Our nightstands and coffee tables hold current reads. There's a system to it, and the system works—as long as I reshelve the books when I'm done with them.

But sometimes I don't. I'm often rushing to finish a literary blog post at the end of a workday or staging golden-hour photo shoots right before I race out the door to pick up my kids from school. In the moment, it doesn't seem like a big deal to leave a few books lying in the sunroom, two rooms away from where they belong. I tell myself I'll pick them up when I get home. But by the time I return home, I've forgotten. Do this for a month or so and the system breaks down, making it difficult to find what I'm looking for. And then when I really need a book, it's nowhere to be found.

To get my literal house in order, and to keep my physical environment from sabotaging me, I often repeat a simple mantra: complete the cycle, which is basically a fancy way of saying "finish what you start." A *Modern Mrs Darcy* blog reader said that in her family, they call this "taking it through the hoop." She says, "All of us are pretty good at getting it *near* the hoop, but the reward is not until it's *through* the hoop." Other readers shared similarly helpful mantras, like "touch it once" and "touch it, complete it," and "do the next step."

The phrase "completing the cycle" resonates with me the most. I begin cycles every day, and you do too. You probably have cycles in progress right now. And generally speaking, we're happier—and a lot tidier—when we complete them. That means we finish what we start, in a more or less prompt way.

Some benefits of complete cycles are obvious. When we don't finish what we start, we lose our important papers. Our clothes may be clean, but they're rumpled in the bottom of the dryer—or worse, hanging in the closet but too wrinkled to wear. We can't make today's breakfast until we clean the skillet from yesterday's eggs.

When we promptly complete our cycles, we get to bypass all kinds of avoidable last-minute emergencies. Take this example from the Bogel household, circa 2016. We finished all our tax paperwork in February and were proud of ourselves for finishing two months early. We felt like it was done, because the hard part was over. But on April 15, we found ourselves frantically searching for the checkbook, then driving across town to the only post office with midnight pickup because though we did the hard part, we never took the final step of putting the forms and our payment in the mail. We were cursing ourselves that night for not completing the cycle.

Completing the cycle isn't a magic bullet. But its benefits are real, even if they aren't all readily apparent. Open cycles consume mental energy, occupy brain space, and beg us to monitor them as "jobs in progress." Our brains get anxious when too many cycles remain open, because it takes energy to maintain them. They register as clutter to our brains. We're using mental energy and our limited working memory trying not to forget about them. Think about it as you would a computer's memory—the more RAM that's available, the smoother the machine operates. When a cycle is complete, that's one less thing to keep track of so we can focus on the task at hand.

You can apply this foundational habit of completing the cycle in a broad range of instances to keep your physical space from sabotaging you. These are some ideas of what this could look like:

- Sorting the mail as soon as you bring it inside
- Paying bills when you receive them
- Putting your keys in a designated spot as soon as you get home
- Filing important papers before they get buried on your desk
- Putting meat in the freezer when you get home from the grocery store
- Putting dirty dishes in the dishwasher instead of setting them on the counter
- Hanging up your coat when you walk in the door
- Putting reusable bags back in the trunk after you return from running errands

- Adding hot sauce to the grocery list when you empty the bottle
- Folding the laundry before wrinkles set in, and then actually putting it away

Clear the Clutter

We tend to think of overthinking as something that happens in our heads, but it's also intimately connected to our physical spaces. Clearing the clutter is a key way to stop overthinking before it starts. We can avoid wasting time and energy looking for our keys and avoid the whole-life meltdown that often accompanies such an occurrence.

Clutter isn't great for mental function, so clear counters do a lot for inner calm. It's easier to forget that important paper if it's buried in a sea of discarded coffee mugs and Scotch tape and the other detritus that tends to accumulate on the kitchen counter.

You don't need to live in a *Martha Stewart Living* spread to reap the benefits of tidying up. If you complete your cycles, your spaces will probably look tidier, but tidiness in and of itself isn't the point. By streamlining your spaces, you can streamline your thought process, and your brain won't have to work so hard to tend to life's details. The point is to maintain a level of organization that allows you to find your stuff when you need it.

I'm easily overwhelmed by messy spaces (although my standards are admittedly low, and I've decided book stacks are *not* in the mess category). These few tricks have helped me gain control of a situation that's gotten out of hand:

- When I can't find something, that's my cue to clean up. I nearly always find what I'm looking for in the process, and approaching the search with purpose keeps me from growing flustered. (Plus, by the time I find my keys, my space functions a lot better because it's tidier.)

- When I'm overwhelmed by the state of disarray, I stake out one clear area. In my office, it's my desk. In the kitchen, it's the island. In my bedroom, it's the bed.
- After I have one clear area, I clean up left to right. I learned this trick from a dystopian literary novel—and it really works. Instead of debating how to tackle the messy space, I move straight to the action stage. And my progress is visible and obvious.

Clutter, by definition, distracts us from what's important and makes it harder to focus on the things that matter. This affects some of us more than others. I have long loved Susan C. Pinsky's book *Organizing Solutions for People with ADHD*, even though I'm not technically in her target audience. She says that to those who find clutter especially distracting, simple is more important than pretty, practical is more important than aspirational, and clutter is deadly. When we don't have our stuff under control, we pay for it with extra effort, time, stress, and money. The less we have, the easier it is to keep things in order. As Pinsky says, "The straightest path to efficiency is reduction."

Don't Duplicate the Work

Saving mental energy means not repeatedly tackling the same tasks. If you can do the work once and enjoy the benefits repeatedly, do it. Don't duplicate the work!

For example, every time I travel, I use the same packing list (that someone else created for me, a strategy we will explore in chapter 9). Prior to working from the list, I felt anxious about forgetting things—probably because I forgot things on a regular basis.

But now my packing list captures the things I used to forget—my toothbrush, mascara, Altoids, literary stickers for book events. I simply tick off the boxes as I load my suitcase and don't worry about omitting essentials, because my list has proven to be dependable.

Take Care of Your Body

When it comes to overthinking, our physical bodies matter. Overthinking is not all in—or about—our headspace. Any plan to prevent excessive overthinking has to consider what's happening in our bodies, because when we take care of our bodies, we take care of our brains as well.

When facing a subject as complex as overthinking, it may seem silly to focus on these physical fundamentals, what Dutch psychiatrist and researcher Bessel van der Kolk calls the "basic housekeeping functions of the body." But that is a trap. Van der Kolk is the author of the fascinating book *The Body Keeps the Score*, about how traumatic experiences manifest themselves in our brains, minds, and bodies, and in his work he's seen time and again that tending to our bodies' foundational needs is essential. He writes, "Breathing, eating, sleeping, pooping, and peeing are so fundamental that their significance is easily neglected when we're considering the complexities of mind and behavior." But we do so at our peril, because the workings of the physical body are intimately tied to the workings of the brain.

Following my own 9/11 experience, one of the first things I did was quit caffeine, because my anxious mind and overtaxed body didn't need additional stimulation. Anyone who's ever lost their temper when hungry or lain awake overthinking in the middle of the night has experienced the tie between the brain and the body. One reason I lost my mind over the immunization certificates was that I was tired. The middle of the night is prime overthinking time for a reason: we're sleepy! We don't do silly things like compulsively check our phones when we're well rested and focused; we do it when we're tired and distracted. The rested mind is less likely to rabbit trail.

Dr. Emmons, author of *The Chemistry of Calm*, counts sleep, exercise, and diet among the "roots of resilience" that equip us to stay calm and emotionally steady, even when facing stress and loss. "If something is bad for the rest of the body," writes Emmons, "it is also bad for the brain." The converse is also true. These strategies make not only our bodies healthy but our brains as well, improving our energy and focus. An energetic and focused mind is not an overthinking mind.

Lack of exercise is tied directly to overthinking. Of exercise, Emmons writes, "Imagine a drug that was inexpensive, had no negative side effects when used properly, helped everyone who used it, prevented most chronic illness, slowed the aging process, improved sleep, reduced stress, protected the brain, lifted mood, boosted self-esteem, and even enhanced one's sex life—it would be more popular than Prozac!" That drug is exercise, and Emmons doesn't mince words about it: "The economics of energy are like good investing: spend it wisely and you will get even more of it. Your best investment is regular exercise, which not only protects the cells but also makes them better energy producers."

We don't need to make this complicated. While some circumstances may call for more precise prescriptions, perhaps involving a physician's input, most of us don't need to overthink caring for our physical bodies. This was hammered home to me not long ago when I went to see my doctor for my annual physical. When I told her I was concerned about my family's medical history, her instructions were so simple I laughed out loud. "You look like you're in good shape," she said. "I tell all my patients to do four things: walk for at least twenty minutes every day, get enough sleep, eat real food, and drink plenty of water."

"That's it?" I asked.

"That's it," she said. "We could talk all day about fine-tuning the details, but if you don't start with these essentials, none of it will matter."

Enough said.

Take Breaks

Thinking is hard work. When we're mentally rested and refreshed, it's easier to keep our thoughts on track. We don't just get tired because we're sleepy; simply maintaining mental focus throughout the day depletes our energy. Because a tired brain easily becomes an overthinking brain, we need to give ourselves mental breaks not just at night but also throughout the day.

We can think well for only so long, no matter what we're thinking about. This is why we all take breaks in the course of normal life—for ten minutes or a few hours or occasionally for days on end. So be smart about it, and give yourself regular, restorative breaks. Be leery of what productivity expert Laura Vanderkam calls "fake breaks," the sorts of habits we mindlessly engage in to fill moments of downtime, like checking email or scrolling through Instagram. These are problematic because we need time to refresh ourselves, not our inbox.

When our energy lags, our bodies and brains need real breaks—things like sitting with a good cup of coffee or popping into the bookstore on your lunch break or, when you're really feeling overwhelmed, sitting quietly and staring at the clouds for a few minutes. On the virtue of "conscious breaks," Vanderkam writes, "Going for a thirty-minute walk at lunch . . . will clear your head and enable focus for the rest of the afternoon. That means you won't get stuck staying late to complete something that has to be done by the end of the day that you haven't gotten to because your addled brain keeps reading the same email six times in a row."

When we're mentally fatigued, overthinking creeps in because our depleted brains are less able to defend against it. That's why on workdays, I like to work in one-and-a-half to two-hour blocks, with short breaks in between. I often take a quick walk around the block and call it a "mental health break." It might sound like a joke, but it's not. Here are some of my favorite things I do on those breaks:

- Read a chapter of a novel (although, as someone who reads for a living, I need to make sure I choose a book that doesn't feel like work)
- Flip through a cookbook or gardening book
- Get the mail and chat with the neighbors
- Phone a friend to check in
- Go for a short run
- Do a five-minute yoga video on YouTube
- Take a walk by myself, with no headphones
- Sit on the porch swing for a few minutes
- Visit the neighborhood bookstore and browse the shelves

Taking breaks sounds simple, but when we think *simple* isn't effective, that's when we start overcomplicating and overthinking. Our strategies don't have to be complex to serve us well.

Get Out of Your Own Way

When I was freaking out about those immunization certificates, any of the strategies in this chapter would have helped me. If I'd neatly filed the papers the day I'd obtained them, I wouldn't have wondered where they were. If I'd completed the cycle by scanning them and sending them to the schools, the task would have been finished. If my desk and counters had been tidier, I wouldn't have assumed the papers were lying around somewhere. If I'd just gone to bed and left it until morning, I would have saved myself a miserable hour and could have dealt with it the next day when I was fresh and well rested.

Here's what I *did* do. I had a good cry about my state of incompetence, read a chapter of the novel in progress on my nightstand, and promptly fell asleep. I woke up the next morning a little embarrassed about my freak-out from the previous evening but with new clarity. I thought I'd last seen those papers in the house, but could they possibly be in the car? I walked outside, still in my pajama pants, and found them right where I'd left them: on the floorboard by the driver's seat, slightly rumpled, because for over a month I'd been dropping my purse on them every time I got in the car.

When it comes to overthinking, you feel powerless when you don't know what to do. Well, these are straightforward habits you can develop to set yourself up for success. They sound simple, because they *are* simple—but don't underestimate their impact. File your papers. Put the breakfast dishes away. And deal with those forms—today. Because with the right habits, you can stop much overthinking before it starts.

·············· Next Steps ··············

1. Which habits serve you well right now? Which habits need some work?

   ....

   ....

   ....

   ....

2. What cycles do you engage in that would be helpful to complete in a timely manner?

   ....

   ....

   ....

   ....

3. Is clutter distracting you from what's important? If yes, where?

   ....

   ....

   ....

   ....

4. Can you identify any tasks that you could complete one time and enjoy the benefits repeatedly, like my packing list? If yes, what are they?

....

....

....

....

5. When it comes to taking care of your body, how would you say you're doing?

....

....

....

....

6. What changes, if any, would you like to make as far as sleep, nutrition, and exercise are concerned?

....

....

....

....

....

7. What are your favorite ways to take real breaks? What
   new breaks might you like to try?

....

....

....

....

Part 2

Take
Charge

6

Speed Up to Move On

Thinking has, many a time, made me sad, darling; but doing never did in all my life. . . . My precept is, "Do something, my sister, do good if you can; but at any rate, do something."

Elizabeth Gaskell

I've ridden a motorcycle once in my life, back in my college days. I wouldn't call myself the adventurous sort. I'd never wanted or planned to ride a motorcycle, but I needed a ride to the airport, and freshmen like myself weren't allowed to have cars on campus. We were, however, allowed to have motorcycles—and my friend Luke, grateful for any excuse to take his bike for a ride, jumped at the chance to make the half-hour trip.

When the day came, I told Luke I was a nervous newbie and asked if he could start off slow, for my sake.

He laughed. "I'm sorry," he said, "but no."

I knew he loved his bike, but still. *How rude.* "Gee, thanks,"
I said.

"Believe me," he said, "it's better this way. If we ride slow, we'll
wobble. You've got to speed up to ride steady. It's like when you
learned to ride a bike as a kid. You may feel uncomfortable at first,
but you'll feel a lot better when we hit the gas and get moving."

He was right. The first few seconds were shaky, but after that,
I *did* enjoy our nice, smooth ride.

Back then I never could have predicted how often I'd think
about that one motorcycle ride in the years to come. You might
expect that my thoughts turn to Luke and that ride whenever I see
two college kids on a bike, but you would be wrong. No, I think
of our trip when I'm slowly and carefully making a decision—
and I see myself wobbling. The memory of that morning's ride
prompts me to ask myself if I'd be better off speeding up.

Waiting Time Is Wasted Time

We all want to make good decisions in life. We may automatically
slow down when facing a big decision because we want to make
sure we're taking it seriously. As I pointed out in chapter 1, purposeful waiting has a place; there are times for slow and methodi-
cal decisions. If you're contemplating how to deal with a difficult
family member, whether you should go back to school, or if you
can afford to buy a house, time may be exactly what you need.

But at a certain point, waiting time becomes wasted time. We
think moving slowly will help us, but we can spend so much time
considering our options that we get stuck in analysis paralysis.
We need to remember that *important* doesn't necessarily require
slow every step of the way. There comes a time when a decision
doesn't need any more thought—and past this point, we're *over*-
thinking it. We don't need to keep pondering; we need to speed
up—that is, make a decision and take some action.

Sometimes it's easy to differentiate between purposeful pondering and overthinking; other times it takes a while to recognize what's going on. But with practice, you'll get better at recognizing when slowing down is a hindrance instead of a help and learn what to do about it.

Here are some signals that it's time to move on.

When Making a Decision between Two Good Choices

Deciding between two good options sounds like a great position to be in, but it's surprisingly tough because there may be no "right" answer and no clear way to decide. Our instinct may be to slow down until the right answer becomes obvious, but we do so at our peril—if we're not careful, we can plunge straight into analysis paralysis. When we're facing two good options, we don't need more time. We need to move on.

Recently, my friend Claire slowed down in order to make a big decision, and it backfired big-time—until she realized what was happening and sped up. Claire has a killer resumé: she was an early employee at Twitter, knows everything about start-ups, and has been successfully running her own business for years. She and I meet regularly with a group of women who also all run their own businesses. We talk through issues we're facing in our work and share ideas and strategies for what to do about them.

Over the course of one long summer, we listened to Claire discuss big-picture decisions she needed to make about her business. She eventually decided her next step would be to hire a consultant, someone who could help her evaluate her work with fresh eyes and determine how to move forward. She'd done her research, asked around, and narrowed her options to two solid candidates who were both competent, comfortable to talk with, and highly recommended. Now it was time to pick one.

This was a big decision for Claire. Everyone in our small group could see what was happening. Claire had already given the matter more than enough consideration. She needed to make a decision, because until she did, her bike was going to wobble.

And so at our next meeting, we invited her to flip a coin. *Right then.* Heads for Coach A, tails for Coach B.

She flipped the coin and hired her coach. (Actually, when the coin came up heads, Claire realized she'd been hoping for tails—so she hired the *other* coach. But she hired one.)

If we recognize that we're debating between two good choices, we just need to choose one—because until we do, we keep the decision always in our mind, preventing us from moving on.

When You Know What to Do but Are Dragging Your Feet

As I started paying more attention to my own patterns of over-thinking, I noticed something surprising. I had assumed that I succumbed to overthinking when I didn't know what to do, but that's often not what's really happening. Sometimes I only pretend I don't know what to do, because *I don't want to do it.* (If you've ever spent twenty minutes lying awake in the middle of the night wondering if you should get out of bed to go to the bathroom, you know what I'm talking about.)

Whether the issue is big or small, if we don't like the answer, we may be tempted to keep searching for a better one—even if a better answer isn't going to arrive. We may not like the answer because we're feeling lazy, or it's not perfect, or we're worried about looking dumb. That doesn't mean it's not the right one. And once we have that answer, we still need to follow through.

We just discussed how needing to choose between two good options can lead to overthinking. Interestingly, facing a choice between two unpleasant options can do the same. In both cases, we need to take action in order to move forward.

Last year when I was traveling for work, I stayed at a hip boutique hotel a few notches above my usual level of accommodations. It was luxurious and spare, the kind of place that has absinthe on the room service menu, with vintage album covers on the walls and retro Victrola speakers on the bar carts.

The bed was comfortable, the pillows were soft, the blackout curtains effective. And yet when I lay down to sleep around midnight, I realized the whole room was vibrating with a deep bass beat. I couldn't hear the music, but I could *feel* it.

I told myself I was too tired for it to matter; I'd fall right asleep.

But I didn't. I tossed and turned and then tried my usual tricks: I got up and washed my face; I fluffed my pillow; I downloaded a white noise app and tried the ocean setting, then gentle rain, all to no avail.

I suspected I should call the front desk, but I didn't want to be a whiner and I wasn't confident they'd be able to help. I didn't know where the music was coming from, and it wasn't actually loud. I was in that half-awake/half-asleep state that is ripe for overthinking. I kept telling myself I'd fall asleep any minute.

I grew increasingly alarmed as the minutes ticked by, hastening the arrival of my early wake-up call. I knew what I needed to do, and I didn't want to do it. But, finally, I picked up the phone and told the front desk everything I knew: "I'm in 610, there's a bass beat that won't quit, I don't know where it's coming from, but I won't be able to sleep until it stops."

The hotel worker apologized and said she'd send security to take care of it. I was skeptical they'd be able to do anything. But three minutes later, it stopped.

I couldn't believe how quickly the fix came and was annoyed with myself for not calling hours earlier—but only for a minute, because once my room stopped vibrating, I fell right to sleep.

That ideal outcome (albeit two hours too late) led me to adopt this if-then rule for future travels: "When in doubt, call the front desk." The benefits of asking for help far outweigh the drawbacks, even though it doesn't always work quite this well. A few months later, I called the front desk at a different hotel after the second group of drunken strangers wandered past my room, singing loudly, after 1:00 a.m. "We're so sorry, we have a lot of wedding parties tonight," the manager told me on the phone. It still wasn't easy to sleep, but I didn't torture myself wondering if I should take action. (Besides finding my earplugs, that is.)

For a more commonplace example, my distaste for shopping sometimes gets me in trouble. I don't enjoy shopping for clothes and avoid it as much as possible. So even if I know I *need* to shop, I postpone decisions about when and where to do so and what exactly to buy. But at a certain point, if I wear holes in the seat of all my jeans, I need to procure new ones. My "strategy" may work temporarily, but it also ensures I'll spend too much attention on something I abhor.

When we put off doing something we don't want to do, we keep the unpleasant thing right in front of us for much longer than we need to. As long as we're contemplating the issue, we're dwelling on the negative. If we're dreading something, we can serve ourselves well by dealing with it sooner rather than later. If we're overthinking something we can actually do something about, the best thing we can do is speed up to move on. Take action as soon as possible.

When You're Tempted to Beat Yourself Up

Sometimes we slow down because while we have moved forward externally, we haven't moved forward mentally or emotionally. It may look like we've sped up, but we're still wobbling on the inside.

Here's what that looked like one June Friday, when an unexpected problem caught me off guard. Fridays are generally calm spots in my weekly rhythm, but the day had been packed with mentally demanding appointments. In fact, the whole week had been bonkers. I was worn out but looking forward to our evening plans. We were having old acquaintances over for dinner for the first time, and I wanted our new guests to feel at ease and had planned accordingly. The house was clean enough, and I had the ingredients for a casual meal ready to go. Our guests call themselves vegetarian-ish, so I'd decided to put my neighbors' garden surplus to good use and make spaghetti squash tacos. I was skeptical when I first encountered the *Smitten Kitchen* recipe, but many years and many dinners later, the vegetarian tacos are a favorite of my meat-eating family and a meal I regularly make for guests.

My final meeting of the afternoon had run terribly long, and it was past time to get dinner started. I prefer to roast the spaghetti squash for the tacos, but it was too hot to turn on the oven, so I turned to the microwave. As I prepped the squash for cooking, piercing it with a paring knife so the steam could vent while it cooked, I noticed how pretty it was—a pale yellow green, with gentle striping, much prettier than the plain yellow ones at the grocery store.

In the microwave, the squash hissed and steamed like usual. But after it cooked for a half hour, at which point it should have been almost done, I was surprised to see it sitting in a large puddle of water. *That's weird*, I thought. When I took it out and gently cut into it, I realized why my squash looked so pretty—I'd spent the last half hour microwaving a melon.

"I am such an idiot," I told my husband. "I can't believe I did something so stupid. Today, of all days!"

"Hey," Will said, "it's fine. Getting all cranky is just going to make you feel bad. You don't need to dwell on this. It's not that big a deal—and it *is* funny, right?"

He was right. I mean, who microwaves a melon? And while I was tempted to berate myself further and wallow in my misfortune, that wouldn't have done anyone any good, especially me. Sometimes we can benefit from evaluating exactly what went wrong so we can know better next time, but there was no need for that—this was never going to happen again. I didn't need to dwell on my mistake; I needed to let go of my irritation and move on.

I turned my attention to what needed to be done. For obvious reasons, I couldn't afford the time to research my options. We needed dinner, and it didn't much matter what kind. Will was heading out the door to pick up all the kids from all the places, so dinner was on me. I opened the pantry, searching for another vegetarian option, but that took more creativity than I was feeling at the moment. I thought about ordering pizza, but we'd promised tacos, and the situation didn't seem as bad as all that. The least mentally taxing option was to stay with the tacos, even though it meant a grocery run. I grabbed the keys and headed for the door, clearly exasperated.

Laughter defuses any situation, and so on my way to the grocery store, I called a friend and told her what I'd done. She laughed hysterically, which helped me regain my sense of perspective. Twenty minutes later (much faster than I'd imagined), I returned with a banana-yellow spaghetti squash that only vaguely resembled the melon I'd microwaved. (I also grabbed extra cheese and crackers, because dinner wasn't going to be ready soon.)

When our friends arrived, we welcomed them in, poured the wine, and settled everyone into the kitchen. We put out chips and guacamole and a more-substantial-than-originally-planned cheese board. When the tacos were ready, we served them up. It was a lovely evening. And *after* dinner was served, we all had a good laugh when I told our friends about my kitchen mishap.

When we know we need to move forward, we must do it with our whole selves—with our actions *and* our minds. As long as we're contemplating the issue, we're dwelling on the negative. Nobody's got time—or headspace—for that.

Don't wallow, don't wobble, move on.

·············· **Next Steps** ··············

1. Can you think of a time when you "wobbled" while making a decision? How could the situation have been different if you had sped up?

....

....

....

....

2. When have you had to make a decision between two good choices? How did you ultimately decide? Are you deciding between two good choices right now?

....

....

....

3. Can you think of a time when you knew what to do but didn't want to do it? What was that experience like? How did you move forward?

....

....

....

4. Do you tend to beat yourself up when you make small mistakes? Do you tend to dwell on what went wrong? Take a moment to think about what you'll do—and what you'll tell yourself—next time you're tempted to berate yourself for a small mistake.

....

....

....

....

7

Tend Your Garden

There is nothing either good or bad, but thinking makes it so.
William Shakespeare

"Tell me what you eat, and I shall tell you what you are," writes the French epicure Jean Anthelme Brillat-Savarin. Well, when it comes to your mind, you are what you *think*.

Our lives reflect what we persistently think about. Where we choose to place our attention directly affects the way we experience the world around us and the people we become. As Winifred Gallagher writes in her excellent book *Rapt*, "Your life is the creation of what you focus on—and what you don't." Gallagher's observation is hard-earned. *Rapt* begins with a cancer diagnosis—of a "particularly nasty, fairly advanced kind"—but upon leaving the hospital, Gallagher has a realization. It would be easy for the disease to monopolize her attention during her treatment, but she could choose to focus on her life instead. And while that year wasn't the best of her life, it wasn't her worst. *That* is the power of focus.

With our thoughts, we make our worlds. This is why two people can experience the same thing in vastly different ways. When we were in high school, a friend and I both lost ten pounds (that we didn't need to lose) during the same semester. We worked out together, but one of us was focused on outward appearances while the other was focused on getting in shape. And, not coincidentally, one of us became cranky and critical through the process, and one of us grew calm and confident. (I won't tell you who was who; it will make me look bad.) Our actions may have looked the same from the outside, but our experiences were quite different—because of where we chose to place our focus.

What we pay attention to affects more than just our inner experience, because those thoughts don't just stay in our heads. What we *think* directly influences what we *feel*; our thoughts and emotions cannot be separated. We cannot just choose to feel happy or relaxed or excited or mellow, because those emotions are rooted in our thoughts. What happens to us is often out of our control. But what we *think* about what happens determines how we *feel*, and subsequently, what we *do* about it.

Because our thoughts cascade into our feelings and actions, what we think about matters. When we nurture positive thoughts, we feel good; when we nurture negative thoughts, we feel bad. The nature of our thoughts directly affects not only the content of our experience but also our quality of life. This isn't value-neutral. When we feel good, we are kinder, more creative, more expansive in our thinking, more open to possibility, and just more pleasant to be around. When we focus on the negative, we not only feel bad but also make ourselves more and more the type of people who overthink, because negativity fuels the mental spin cycle.

If we think positive thoughts, we're more likely to take positive action. This doesn't mean we have to be thrilled when unwanted things happen, but it does mean there are helpful and unhelpful ways to think about a situation. If we think negative thoughts, we're less likely to take satisfying action.

You Get to Choose What You Think About

Here's the important thing: you get to choose what you think about! This was a revelation when I first read *Renovation of the Heart* fifteen years ago, by philosopher and theologian Dallas Willard. In it he writes, "What we feel and think is (or can and should be) to a very large degree a matter of choice in competent adult persons, who will be very careful about what they allow their mind to dwell upon or what they allow themselves to feel." It may not feel like a choice, but sources both sacred and secular agree that while we can't perfectly control what we feel and think, we have more power than we give ourselves credit for.

And not only can we do it, but if we want to spend less time overthinking and more time thinking about the things that matter to us, we *must* learn to tend our thoughts with care. For this, I've come to embrace a metaphor I first encountered in Gallagher's book *Rapt*. She recommends you treat your mind "as you would a private garden and [be] as careful as possible about what you introduce and allow to grow there." We must learn to tend our own gardens.

Many of us, not realizing the vast impact our thoughts have on our lives, don't pay much mind to the garden we're cultivating. This is a mistake. Attention is powerful, and we can use ours for good or ill. Our thoughts can be our allies or our enemies. We can focus on our fears, our worries, how others have wronged us. We can, in true perfectionist style, focus on the small things we screwed up, the ways we fell short. We can replay unpleasant conversations and unfortunate situations in our minds. Because our thoughts drive our feelings, we can have a pretty good life and still feel miserable. Or, as Gallagher and countless others have discovered, we can face unpleasant circumstances and still experience peace and joy. It all depends on what we choose to focus on.

John Milton writes, "The mind is its own place, and in itself / Can make a heav'n of Hell, a hell of Heav'n." By choosing our thoughts with care, we can cultivate a garden we actually want to spend time in.

What to Do If Your Brain Gets Stuck on the Bad Stuff

Great, you may be thinking. *I've been trying to choose my thoughts with care, and it's not working so well.* What do we do when it feels like we can't choose our thoughts because our brain is stuck in the spin cycle of overthinking—and we don't know how to get free?

In this book, we've been defining overthinking broadly—as repetitive, unhealthy, and unhelpful thoughts that make us feel bad while accomplishing nothing. Now we're going to home in on a specific type of overthinking called *rumination,* so called because the repetitive thinking it describes is similar to the digestive process of animals classified as ruminants, such as cows, that rechew their food to aid in digestion. Rumination may be good for cattle, but for us, nothing good comes of mulling over unworthy issues at length. Instead, rumination hijacks our focus and makes us miserable. When we ruminate, we can't shut off our brains. Our thoughts go round and round; we feel stuck, like a hamster on a wheel. These negative thoughts—and resultant emotions—damage both our ability to think clearly and our general sense of well-being.

When we ruminate, we focus on our problems in an unhelpful way. If we were focusing on *solving* our problems, that would serve us well. But that's not what we do when we ruminate. We go over and over the problem, without searching for a solution. And when we think negative thoughts, we feel bad feelings. This is why rumination is deadly; it affects how we feel and then, subsequently, what we do.

Rumination not only prevents us from solving our problems but also causes its own problems. When we ruminate, we generate worry and anxiety out of proportion to the matter at hand, and then we may even begin to overthink our overthinking. The worst part is that much of this inner agony is wholly unnecessary.

Left unchecked, the situation grows worse over time. The more we overthink, the more we reinforce those thought patterns, making it that much harder to extricate ourselves. If we've been overthinking for decades, we've effectively been blowing dandelion seeds all over our garden, then fertilizing the weeds.

It doesn't have to be this way. Change is possible; we can learn to reinforce positive thought habits. We can learn to better control our attention, although to do so, we may need to experiment.

Strategies to Interrupt Overthinking the Moment It Happens

How do you overcome a lifetime of overthinking? How can you learn to redirect your thoughts to more fruitful pathways? Make a plan for what to do when these thoughts pop up—because they *will* pop up. You need strategies to interrupt rumination when it happens, to eradicate negative thoughts and put a stop to the overthinking. Over time, you'll learn how to make smart decisions about which thoughts to weed out and which to fertilize. As you consciously create new neural pathways, you will be better equipped to stop overthinking in the moment and also become the kind of person who overthinks less. And that feels really good.

Putting a stop to the overthinking you've nurtured for so long won't be easy, but over time your ability to direct your attention will strengthen. You'll begin to reclaim control over your thoughts and, as a result, your feelings and actions. By reinforcing new and healthier patterns of thought, these strategies literally rewire your brain. This isn't a quick fix; putting overthinking to bed is hard work. I've been working on this for years, and I still catch myself overthinking. But because of these strategies, I feel equipped to deal with the negative thoughts when they do pop up.

With the exception of the first, these strategies do not need to be employed in order; feel free to experiment and see which ones work best for you.

Pay Attention to Your Thoughts

You can't change anything until you notice you're doing it, so the first step is to observe what you're thinking about. Where do you habitually direct your focus? Does your mind automatically notice the negative in any situation? What subjects do you unhelpfully dwell on?

Pay attention to your thoughts, including how you talk to yourself—both out loud and in your own head. No one likes to be around someone who constantly spews negativity, and that remains true when you're the one alone with your thoughts.

Here's an example from the writing life. Sometimes (a lot of times) writing is hard. When I grow discouraged by how difficult the process is, I've made it a habit to remember this line from one of my favorite books, *Crossing to Safety*: "Hard writing makes easy reading." This simple mantra reminds me that it's okay for the process to be difficult, and it will ultimately end well—if I keep working hard. This positive self-talk helps me keep my chin up and prompts me to get back to work instead of wasting my mental energy focusing on how hard the process is.

Look for the Good

When you ruminate, your brain gets stuck in a negative thought spiral. Once you're attending to the negative, it's easy to keep doing it. But if you notice what you're doing, you can disrupt rumination by looking for a positive interpretation. And by proactively focusing on the good, you can avoid rumination altogether, because a steady focus harbors few interruptions.

You may have heard of John Gottman, the famed marriage counselor, researcher, and therapist known for his ability to predict with astonishing accuracy if a couple will divorce after observing them in conversation for a mere five minutes. He says it's important that couples learn how to notice and share—*on purpose*—the things they like and appreciate about each other, and to do so in intentional and consistent ways. This sounds simple, but the exercise of seeking out the good has enormous power, and not just in romantic relationships—because unless you're actively looking for the good, it might escape your conscious notice. Train yourself to appreciate the positive.

Another way to look for the good is to practice gratitude. A regular gratitude practice does wonders for overthinking, because it takes your focus off yourself and directs it outward. Gratitude automatically directs your attention to the good stuff, instead of the things you lack or the ways you (or others) fall short. As a bonus, thinking grateful thoughts makes you feel happy. To make gratitude a habit, Gottman's organization, the Gottman Institute, suggests setting a reminder on your phone that prompts you to name something you're grateful for. Eventually, your mind will make this a habit and come to look for the good without prompting. And when you spend more time feeling grateful, you waste less time overthinking.

You can also look for the good to alter your perspective. I frequently rely on this strategy when I'm driving, because it would be all too easy to assume negative intentions for the questionable decisions other drivers make behind the wheel. When someone runs a red light, I always say, out loud, "Maybe there's a woman in labor in the back seat." My kids tease me about this, saying, "Mom, *really*?" But I don't care. Telling myself that the driver may be in a hurry for a good reason helps me remain gracious instead of getting angry. That keeps me focused on being a kind and compassionate human (and an alert driver) instead of har-rumphing about the idiots on the road. You can't control what happens in life, but you can control how you choose to interpret things. When I choose to look for a positive interpretation, I'm nurturing good thoughts instead of unhelpfully dwelling on bad ones.

Consider a Different Point of View

Once your brain lands on a negative interpretation of some-thing—say, your friend left the meeting early because she didn't want to talk to you, everyone is giving you strange looks because you have lipstick on your teeth, your boss called because she's unhappy with your job performance—it's difficult to stay objec-tive. And when you lose objectivity, you head straight for the negative, and stay there.

When your brain gets stuck, you can consciously prompt yourself to consider a different point of view. This exercise in creativity forces you to get out of your own head, and with a bit of distance, you can see your own situation more objectively and lessen the power of the initial thought. Even a neutral interpreta-tion is leagues better than a negative one.

Your alternate interpretation doesn't have to be brilliant. The power comes from simply considering another point of view, because it forces your thoughts off the negative track they're on. What if your friend left the meeting early because she had a dentist appointment? What if people are surprised to see you at the meeting because they thought you were still on vacation? What if your boss called because you left a file on your desk?

When I'm struggling to find a positive—or even neutral—interpretation, I turn to two questions that have consistently helped me get my thinking back on track.

1. *What would I tell my best friend if she were in this situation?*
   When you imagine you're advising someone else, you automatically see the situation more objectively.
2. *What would I like about this if I liked it?* or *What would I consider to be good here, if I considered this to be good?*
   For example: "If I felt that meeting was a success, what reasons would I give?" or "If I thought that conversation went well, why would I think so?"

These questions are effective because they give you needed distance from your own visceral experience and challenge you to engage in the creative exercise of finding another interpretation.

Brush It Aside, for Now

I learned this trick from a yoga-instructor friend: if (or perhaps I should say, *when*) unhelpful thoughts pop up, you don't have to nurture them. When you notice your mind drifting off in a dangerous direction, just tell those thoughts "not now" and brush them aside. My friend suggested I visualize brushing them away, as if I were brushing lint off my sweater.

Here's a low-key example: when I'm writing, I'll have flitting thoughts that say things like, *This is crap!* or *Are you sure you know what you're doing?* I used to engage these thoughts and wrestle with them. But that didn't help anything; instead, it diverted my attention from where it belonged and made me feel bad. Now when I notice these thoughts floating by, I brush them aside, telling myself that they don't matter right now. Then I can refocus my attention on the thing that does matter: actually writing.

Of course, if I choose to catch these thoughts, pull them close, and nurture them, I would have a whole different experience—and not a good one.

My friend Beth gave me similar advice for my work life. In my business, leisurely seasons of creative planning and preparation alternate with busier seasons of execution. In seasons of execution, I'm focused on executing plans I've already made, not on thinking deeply about the big picture—but that doesn't stop me from recognizing issues that need to be dealt with, whether those are about the overall state of my business or finer details of a project in process. Beth taught me that the time to make big decisions is when I'm planning and preparing. And when I'm busy executing those plans—well, that time should be devoted to execution. Now when a big-picture decision presents itself during a season dedicated to execution, I do what Beth taught me: I tell myself, *Execution mode, not decision mode*, capture the idea to address later, and move on. Trusting that I will return to it when the time is right helps me move on in the moment.

Ignore Invalid or Unhelpful Thoughts

In *Almost Everything*, Anne Lamott writes about her ongoing struggle with intrusive thoughts and the only three words that have ever helped her deal with them. Once she was on a North African cliff with a kind Coptic minister and had to make this embarrassing confession: "I promised my psychiatrist I would tell whomever I was with when I was in any high place that since childhood, whenever I'm very, very high up, I think about jumping."

Of the minister, Lamott says, "He didn't miss a beat. Waving away my concern, he said, 'Oh, who doesn't?'"

Lamott relates that his response was exactly right. It made her feel better, and it was *true*. She explains that she isn't depressed or suicidal but nevertheless has these unwelcome thoughts sometimes. The minister's response empowered her to brush them aside.

The vast majority of us have intrusive thoughts like this from time to time, ideas we don't consciously create and that don't represent our true thoughts and feelings. In their excellent book *Overcoming Unwanted Intrusive Thoughts*, Dr. Sally N. Winston and Dr. Martin N. Seif define unwanted intrusive thoughts as "uninvited thoughts that jump into the mind and do not seem to be part of the ongoing flow of intentional thinking." If you have an unwanted intrusive thought yourself—like Lamott's thoughts to jump from high places—you may be concerned, knowing that your life reflects what you persistently think about. Rest assured that not every thought that flits through your head speaks to your underlying character.

It's a mistake to give all your thoughts equal weight. Some thoughts do not deserve to be taken seriously, so don't dignify them with a response. That only serves to empower them, because the effort you use to combat the unwanted intrusive thought only serves to strengthen it. "The simple truth is that what you resist tends to persist."

Instead of choosing to nurture those unwanted thoughts, simply choose to notice them, and let them float away.

Schedule Time to Overthink

The brain likes to have a system it can trust, so give it one. Johnny Cash famously included worry on his personal to-do list (along with "pee" and "call mama"). It sounds silly, but this counterintuitive strategy actually works. If you schedule time every day to worry or overthink, your brain is less likely to nag you with those thoughts throughout the day.

In 13 *Things Mentally Strong Women Don't Do*, therapist Amy Morin reports that many of her therapy clients have found this much-recommended strategy to be effective. "Rather than allowing their worrisome thoughts to affect every waking hour, they find they're sufficiently able to contain their worrying to a specific portion of the day."

When you schedule time to overthink, you may be able to trade fifteen minutes of concentrated overthinking for twenty-three hours and forty-five minutes of relief. Give yourself permission to indulge these thoughts for a limited time period—and set a timer when you begin so those thoughts don't spill into the rest of your day. This keeps the dandelions from taking over the whole garden.

Write It Down

It's easy to build things up in your mind to be much bigger than they actually are. Sometimes I'll notice I'm feeling completely overwhelmed because it seems like I have so much to do, but when I stop to capture my swirling thoughts—or even better, my action items—in writing, it doesn't look so bad.

This strategy works because it allows us to wrangle our unwieldy thoughts into a more manageable format, which restores our objectivity. This is old advice, but it remains useful. Many things don't feel so daunting once they are written down, because the act of writing forces us to clarify what's actually happening and what we need to do about it.

Many find writing to be a helpful tool, but watch out. Morin calls journaling a "common trap" for those inclined to ruminate. She writes, "For overthinkers, journaling may backfire. If you write about bad things that happen, things you worry about, or uncomfortable emotions you experience, your journal may reinforce your negative thoughts." If you relate, Morin's advice for your journaling sessions is to stick to the facts rather than dwell on the emotions surrounding them.

You can take this a step further by writing down your negative thoughts, ripping up the paper, and throwing away the pieces. An old coach of mine once had our team perform this exercise before we began our practices. We'd write down our negative thoughts on paper, ball them up, and physically toss them in the trash can. I was skeptical at the time, but science was on my coach's side, because the symbolic action seems to convince your brain that the matter has been dealt with.

Distract Yourself

We may discount distraction because it seems juvenile. Shouldn't you reject negative thoughts outright instead of encouraging your mind to simply wander away from them? The answer is *no*. If the strategy keeps you from indulging in overthinking, then it's effective. And distraction *works*.

Think of it like riding out a craving. Studies indicate that the average food craving lasts only three to five minutes. If you can avoid the craving for that short period of time, the trigger food often doesn't look enticing just a few minutes later. The same holds true for overthinking. Nolen-Hoeksema writes, "Giving people positive distractions from their overthinking for just eight minutes is remarkably effective in lifting their moods and breaking their cycle of repetitive thought."

Distraction works because the mind can only do so many things at once, so when negative thoughts beckon, find another way to keep your mind occupied. Read a book, call a friend, pay a bill, play eight minutes of Tetris.

Move Your Body to Move Your Mind

One of the most effective distractions involves physically moving your body. To change what's happening in your mind, a change of scenery literally changes your perspective. Nolen-Hoeksema has found that prolonged movement not only gives you something else to focus on but also boosts energy levels, reduces stress, pumps blood to the brain, and improves mood. For maximum effectiveness, choose an exercise that requires you to concentrate on what you're doing. For example, a long-distance runner could easily overthink while moving down familiar sidewalks, but running trails is more mentally demanding, and thus better for crowding out overthinking.

A twenty-minute exercise session may be most effective, but don't let that stop you from exploring little fixes. When your brain is stuck, try moving your body—walk the dog, take out the trash, do jumping jacks or burpees, clean the kitchen, rake leaves, climb the stairs, dance to a song you love. To get unstuck, get moving.

You Can Harness Your Thoughts

While you can't perfectly control what your mind dwells on, you have a great deal of freedom to choose your thoughts—and that control will grow stronger with practice as you establish new mental habits and neural pathways. Harnessing your thoughts is not easy, and it may take time to see results. But it's possible, and it's worth it.

Make a plan for when those negative thoughts pop up. Begin by paying attention to your thoughts. What have you been focusing on this week? What topics have been prompting you to ruminate? Which strategies are you going to use to do something about it?

You don't have to be at the mercy of your negative thoughts. Choose a few strategies from this chapter that look promising to you, and when rumination strikes again, try a new experiment and see what happens.

·············· Next Steps ··············

1. When you pay attention to your thoughts, what do you notice? Where do you habitually direct your focus? What sends you into the overthinking spin cycle?

   ....

   ....

   ....

2. A regular gratitude practice does wonders for overthinking. Pause a moment to list three things you're grateful for.

   ....

   ....

   ....

3. Can you think of a situation that's troubling you right now? What would you tell your best friend to do if they were in that situation?

   ....

   ....

   ....

   ....

4. In this chapter, I share two mantras I rely on: "Hard writing makes easy reading" and "Execution mode, not decision mode." Do you have any mantras you rely on? Can you think of any you would like to adopt?

....

....

....

....

5. What's your plan for when negative thoughts pop up? Which strategies are you going to try when that happens? List them here.

....

....

....

....

8

Limit Yourself
to Free Yourself

*Habits gradually change the face of one's life as time changes
one's physical face; and one does not know it.*

Virginia Woolf

One dreary winter, my friend Lori talked me into attending
barre class with her at six o'clock in the morning. Despite
having to drag myself out of bed well before dawn on freezing-
cold mornings, I quickly took to the routine of it and was surprised how much I enjoyed it.

The 6:00 a.m. crew contained a fair number of people who
rushed out the door when class ended because they needed to
shower, change, and get to work. I, on the other hand, rarely need
to look polished by 8:00 a.m. Most days I could work in yoga

pants—or even pajamas—if I wanted to. I didn't linger afterward, but I wasn't in a rush.

My favorite part of class was the cooldown at the end. I enjoyed—and needed—the stretching and breath work; it's good for both flexibility and getting centered for the day to come. But one thing about the cooldown consistently made me anxious. During the last minutes of class, the instructor would tell everyone that if we needed to leave five minutes early, no worries, we could. We showed up, we did the hard part, and now it would be fine to slip out the door and get on with our day.

She meant well, but her kind encouragement to do whatever worked for us always got my mental gears whirring. *Should I or shouldn't I?* In the midst of our breathing and stretching, the instructor had introduced a choice where no choice existed. *Stop it,* I would tell myself, *I have the time I need.* But I nevertheless found her invitation tempting. I'm always eager to steal a few extra minutes, and she was offering. Why not rush away and use that time for the next thing on my list? And so I'd lay on my back, still stretching, but now focused on the door instead of my breath, jealous of the people who had taken her up on her offer to leave early, and wondering if I should have been one of them.

That all changed the day I realized that while the instructor was offering me a choice, I didn't need to accept her offer—or even consider it. *Don't overthink it, Anne,* I told myself. *You already decided to be here. So be here.*

And just like that, the pressure to make a decision was gone.

Why It's Important to Limit Your Options

Deciding whether to cut a workout short by a few minutes is a little thing, but these little decisions add up. Each decision we make throughout the day takes a toll on our finite amount of mental energy—what to have for breakfast, which route to take to work, how to handle a tricky conversation, whether to buy new jeans before the sale ends, how our child will get home from practice on Friday. Each small decision requires only a bit of brain power, but the cumulative effect is large.

The more choices we encounter, the more likely we are to succumb to decision fatigue—that state where, exhausted from making decision after decision, our ability to choose breaks down. Unless we're on guard, we may not consciously notice decision fatigue creeping in. When we're physically tired, we know it— we can tell when we're short on sleep or worn out from a hard workout because we *feel* it in our bodies. But decision fatigue is sneaky. Instead of feeling specifically tired in a certain way, we feel overwhelmed.

To avoid decision fatigue, it helps to think of our mental energy as we would a budget—or more aptly, a per diem. We can't make decision after decision without paying a price. The more decisions we make in a day, the worse the quality of our decisions will be over time. Our mental capacity to tackle them erodes and we start to overthink. Conversely, the more decisions we eliminate, the longer we'll retain our decision-making capacity throughout the day.

When we overthink our decisions all day long, we consume more mental energy and experience decision fatigue sooner. And once we feel overwhelmed, getting our thoughts under control is more difficult. As we've seen, it's a vicious cycle.

To stay out of the mental weeds, you can implement your own mental conservation plan, consciously reducing the mental energy you regularly expend by streamlining decisions and creating routines. Choreographer Twyla Tharp, who says her own life is "all about repetition," calls these preestablished, repeatable routines "automatic but decisive patterns of behavior." Their beauty is that by giving you less to think about, they make it easier for you to get the important things done.

Many of us resist routine because it feels confining or boring. I can appreciate that, because I instinctively prefer abundant options and an open calendar to a regimented schedule. But *boring* doesn't have to be a bad thing. Predictability can be exactly what we need, because the purpose of routine is not to limit us but to clear away the mental clutter. "A solid routine fosters a well-worn groove for one's mental energies and helps stave off the tyranny of moods," writes Mason Currey in his book *Daily Rituals*, about the working habits of 243 renowned artists. Routines are meant to serve us, not handcuff us. When smartly deployed, these option-limiting strategies create freedom by creating headspace, whether we're making museum-worthy art or just trying to manage our ordinary days.

Strategies to Streamline Decisions

Let's explore some specific strategies you can establish to limit your options and streamline recurring decisions. Some are obvious; others may surprise you. All have the common goal of establishing habits that make it harder for overthinking to slip in. Think of them not as handcuffs but as your default settings. In lieu of a pressing need to make a different choice, the "boring" routines you create can serve as a fatigue-busting framework. Because you already decided these things once, you don't have to decide every time you're presented with the same question.

Eat the Same Thing

It's remarkable how many decisions we face every day about food. Food and mealtimes play a huge role in our rhythms of life, so when we streamline these things, we save big.

The first time I realized it's okay to eat the same thing every day was ten years ago, when I went through an intense (and brief) CrossFit stage. I quickly realized that many of our gym's elite performers ate the same thing every day, and I mean the *exact* same thing. One of my training buddies ate turkey, green beans, and almonds, measured to the ounce, six or seven mini-meals per day. Some athletes would mix things up by adding variety for dinner or implementing a weekend cheat day, but to me, the backbone of their diets seemed mind-numbingly boring. Nevertheless, they sang its praises, saying the mental savings generated by this consistency were nothing short of amazing.

When I started paying attention, I realized they weren't alone. Many high performers in a variety of disciplines regularly eat the same thing every day to free up mental space. I wasn't trying to run the world or even hit a new personal record in the gym, but I liked the idea of preserving my mental energy for loftier things than my lunch menu.

Flash forward ten years, and to my great surprise, I've become one of *those* people. Ninety percent of my days, breakfast and lunch look the same, day in and day out. Breakfast is some combination of eggs and avocados. Lunch is red curry in cold weather, huge salads in warmer months. It's not *exactly* the same thing, but it's close; the formula is easy to make, easy to shop for, and easy to vary.

If the idea of eating the exact same thing every day makes you queasy, relax. You can implement the same principle in less dramatic ways. For years I planned our family dinners around the Kroger sale flyers, which dramatically reduced our choices. If chicken breasts and salmon were on sale, we'd eat chicken breasts and salmon. Later, I further limited our options by creating a meal matrix. It's not a set-in-stone menu but a template that narrows our options, embracing meatless Mondays, taco Tuesdays, and pizza Fridays.

Whether you choose to eat the exact same thing or adopt a starting point like a meal matrix, you'll save significant amounts of mental energy.

Adopt a Signature Dish

When I was twenty-two years old, I read that everyone should have a signature dish—a reliable recipe you're always prepared to make for friends. That way, you don't have to spend your mental energy deciding what to serve, and you don't have to worry about choosing or executing a new recipe when guests come over. Instead, you can fall into your regular routine—at least as far as the food is concerned—and focus on your friends.

Over the years, I've enjoyed observing how various friends put this concept into practice. Once I stayed with my friend Lisa right after she'd hosted a fancy dinner for eighteen—and not just hosted but *prepared and served.* Lisa is a born hostess and past hospitality professional, so I was interested in the practicalities of the situation. What did she serve, and how did she pull off a party for such a large crowd?

She always serves the same thing for fancy dinners, she told me, because she has enough to worry about without stressing about the food. Her signature menu is beef tenderloin (roasted in the oven, with homemade horseradish sauce), Caesar salad (with doctored store-bought dressing, and you better believe I photographed the bottle for later reference when she pulled it out of the fridge to show me), twice-baked Boursin cheese potatoes, and dessert from a local bakery. Guests love the meal because it's delicious; Lisa loves it because she's made it so many times she doesn't have to think about it.

I've never hosted a fancy dinner party, but the same principle applies to casual gatherings. At my house, one of the key reasons we're comfortable having people over is that we know what we're making, and we know it's easy. My first signature dish was chicken Parmesan, but as I've gotten older, my go-to dishes have gotten simpler. These days, we love a good taco night for large crowds and street-cart chicken for smaller ones. Cozy winter nights call for pot roast in the Dutch oven. For a laid-back menu, we serve nachos (cheap) or sushi (splurge). For dessert, I rely on an almost-flourless chocolate cake I've made so many times I know the recipe by heart. If I want a sweet treat with a casual feel, I bake the Barefoot Contessa's Outrageous Brownies, which are always a crowd-pleaser.

Having people over is a reliable way to deepen your relationships, but it can also feel daunting, simply because of the practicalities. Choosing a signature dish in advance gives you one less thing to think about, so you can trust that the food won't be the obstacle to seeing friends.

Wear the Same Thing

When I was in high school, I envied my Catholic school friends who wore the same skirt, polo, and cardigan to school every day. When they rolled out of bed every morning they knew exactly what they would wear. To my high school self, that meant they could sleep for the extra fifteen minutes I spent choosing my outfit each morning. My friends' tight parameters meant a streamlined decision-making process.

As I grew older, I became fascinated by people who not only choose to wear the same thing every day but do so explicitly because they want to make things easier for themselves. Even former President Obama, spurred by the research on decision fatigue, chose to wear only gray or blue suits while in office. "I'm trying to pare down decisions," he told Michael Lewis in a *Vanity Fair* interview. "I don't want to make decisions about what I'm eating or wearing. Because I have too many other decisions to make."

It's not just schoolgirls and the fashion-averse who employ uniforms. Many stylish people, including ones who work in the fashion industry, also embrace the personal uniform, which surprised me at first. Wouldn't fashionable people relish getting dressed each day? But their reasoning makes sense—if you try to keep up with the trends, you could lose your mind, along with a whole lot of mental energy. As long ago as 1977, the late Carrie Donovan, who served as editor at *Vogue* and *Harper's*, wrote, "The truly well-organized women have worked out a sort of 'uniform' way of putting themselves together attractively but efficiently." For decades, she urged people to "develop a uniform for yourself that works." Donovan's own uniform involved all black, plus huge eyeglasses and bold accessories. Grace Coddington, who served as *Vogue's* creative director for twenty-five years, also came to embrace wearing only black, saying, "I don't want to think about what I'm wearing in the morning; I want to put all of my focus on the clothes I'm shooting. It's like a uniform. You don't have to make a decision about it. I spend my whole life making decisions."

Though I admired people who boldly committed to a single daily uniform, I never thought I could be one of them. It felt too extreme for my tastes. But then one summer I noticed that I had accidentally fallen into a uniform of my own. Since I had to get dressed every day no matter what, I unconsciously made it easier for myself. Every day I wore a striped shirt (one of a dozen slightly different designs), neutral bottoms, and silver sandals. I loved it, because I rolled out of bed knowing exactly what I would wear that day: the next shirt hanging in my closet and whatever bottoms happened to be clean.

Even if you don't wish to wear only striped shirts till the end of your days, a clothing matrix can serve the same function as a food matrix. Many of my own outfits are variations on a theme, like my oft-repeated "column" of a dark top with jeans, plus a pendant necklace. A less-drastic iteration is the "capsule wardrobe," which has been popular in recent years, or the "ten-item wardrobe," which Jennifer L. Scott unpacks in her delightful book *Lessons from Madame Chic,* in a chapter tellingly called "Liberate Yourself with the Ten-Item Wardrobe." All do their job by limiting your choices so your brain space can be allocated for other things.

Adopt a Signature Look

Just like a signature dish, one fancy outfit can fulfill a multiplicity of roles.

When Will and I got married, I found a little black dress for our rehearsal dinner on the sale rack at Ann Taylor: raw silk, thin straps, A-line to just below the knee. In other words, it's incredibly versatile and appropriate for countless occasions. I used to wonder if it was okay to wear the same dress *again,* but I decided a decade ago to just go with it. We recently celebrated our nineteenth anniversary, so this dress has been to a hundred weddings and cocktail parties by now.

It's still timeless and still looking good—and until it finally wears out, I'm going to keep wearing it everywhere.

Limit Yourself to One Source

We all have decisions we can't automate because they just don't come up that often. For example, in recent months I've needed to choose new storage bins for my pantry, find a new kennel for my dog, Daisy, and hire a speaker for a community event. Because I'm not accustomed to making them, these decisions, while infrequent, can eat up vast amounts of mental energy. I don't do any of these things regularly, so I'm a novice. And because I like to learn new things, I can needlessly overinvestigate my options in any new-to-me situation.

That's why, when facing decisions like these—ones I've never made before and may never make again—I've decided in advance to proactively limit my options. One of my preferred ways to do that is by limiting myself to just one source. I established this personal policy a few years ago, after I learned my lesson shopping for new bedding. Since I'm not fond of shopping, I'd postponed the decision for too long and finally reached the point where I needed to buy some—and fast. When I started looking online, I was quickly overwhelmed by the choices. I needed *enough* options, not *infinite* ones!

I explained my predicament to my interior-decorator friend and asked her to tell me just one store where I could find what I was looking for. She obliged (her answer: Pottery Barn), which brought my limitless options back into the reasonable range. She gave me a further head start by highlighting a few duvets she thought would look good in my bedroom. With drastically reduced options, it took me five minutes to decide. Not hours.

Now, whenever the countless options feel overwhelming, I look for a way to quickly narrow my options. Not sure what to read next? Try limiting yourself to the books already on your shelf or those available right now at your regular library branch. Need a birthday gift? Try limiting yourself to just one store (or even just one category, like journals). Not sure what to plant in this year's herb garden? You guessed it: instead of driving all over town to see what's available, resolve to plant only what you can find at one local nursery.

Limit Yourself to One Time

If you find yourself constantly thinking about how to fit something into your schedule or when to fit it in, limiting your options by establishing a set time can help. Committing to a set time is hard for some of us (me included), but once that time is set, you don't have to think about it anymore. If you decide to work out every other morning at 8:00 a.m., you'll no longer worry about when to squeeze in a workout. If you decide to walk the dog in the hour before dinner, you'll no longer wonder when a good time might be. If you decide Thursday is grocery day, you won't waste mental energy deciding when to run to the store.

If it doesn't work to commit to a set time or you'd prefer not to, you could implement if-then rules to make sure the things you want to do get done without your having to think about them. This strategy works because it anchors a new behavior—one you have to think about—into an existing routine. Over time, your routine expands to accommodate the new behavior. For instance, now if I drink a cup of coffee, I also pour a glass of water. If I heat up food in the microwave, I do a plank until the timer dings. If I brush my teeth, I take two extra minutes and do my stretches. Decide once, and you can repeat these actions forever.

Limit Technology Creep

We can't talk about limiting our options without talking about smartly managing our relationship with technology—because if we're not careful, our handy little devices can take over our lives.

Technology has radically changed the way we live. It brings with it many benefits, yet it also astronomically increases the decisions available to us. When we're choosing something like bedding, we can hop online and encounter far more options than our parents' generation ever could have. The question is not just what kind of information we'll find on our device but whether and how much we will use it. If we carry a device with us, we are constantly deciding (although we often don't realize we're doing this) whether to open our computer or check our phone or refresh our email. As Barry Schwartz writes in his excellent book *The Paradox of Choice,* in which he advocates for fewer options, "You now have the opportunity to choose whether to work every minute of every day, no matter where you are. Even if you turn all your machines off, you think about them! The pressure is always on."

If we're not careful, our devices will clamor for our attention, even if that's exactly what we *don't* want. And every time they do, we will need to *decide* to say yes—or no. Limit those constant recurring decisions by setting smart guidelines now.

Are you constantly asking yourself if now would be a good time to pull out your device? Consider implementing device-free zones in your life—a physical space and/or a set time when you put your device away. When we went camping in the Smokies last summer, we didn't have a whisper of cell service, so I put my phone in the glove compartment. I didn't realize how often I thought about checking my phone until checking it wasn't an option.

When we notice the decisions technology thrusts on us, we can choose to limit them. Take the open tabs on your computer, which often represent unmade decisions. Are they open because you're deciding what to do about them? Take the too-common retailer sales emails. J.Crew is hoping you'll open the email and decide to shop. If you don't want to shop, you must decide to delete (or save for later, which might be worse!). Want to skip those decisions altogether? Unsubscribe from those emails.

Our digital devices can do us a world of good, but they can also encourage decision fatigue. Be smart about how you engage, lest your device become the boss of you instead of the other way around.

Not a Checklist

Many of us resist routines because we fear they will feel confining, but when smartly deployed, they create freedom. You can make only so many decisions in a day, so look for ways to clear away your mental clutter, remembering that "clutter" is relative. If you love clothes, then please enjoy the creative act of getting dressed each morning. If you love to unwind by making elaborate weeknight dinners, go ahead.

The strategies in this chapter are not intended to be a checklist. You don't need to implement them all to reap the benefits. But you can make only so many decisions in one day, and you need mental energy available for the important ones. Think about where you can save by streamlining.

When you take control of recurring decisions, you take control of your headspace. Choose well.

············· Next Steps ·············

1. On a scale of 1 (a little) to 10 (a lot), how much do you currently struggle with decision fatigue?

2. What routines do you currently rely on? What do you appreciate most about them?

   ....

   ....

   ....

3. What new routine would you like to implement?

   ....

   ....

   ....

4. Name one area of your life where you feel you would benefit from consciously limiting your choices. How might you do so?

   ....

   ....

   ....

   ....

5. Do you feel technology is currently spurring you to overthink? What steps can you take to limit technology creep?

....

....

....

....

9

Get Someone Else to Do It

We think that we have to learn how to give, but we forget about accepting things, which can be much harder than giving.

Alexander McCall Smith

When I began the process of launching my literary podcast *What Should I Read Next?*, I realized that podcasting required technical skills I didn't have. I faced a choice: I could learn how to set up hosting, install equipment, edit audio, and compress files myself, or I could hire someone else to do the technical work so I could focus on the creative, nontechnical aspects of making a great show. And if I got someone else to do it, I could retain the bandwidth to keep writing books and blog posts and creating bookish classes.

So I hired my friend and fellow podcaster Knox McCoy to talk me through proof of concept, teach me about advertising possibilities, and guide me in equipment choices. He'd already learned how to do all this; I didn't see the point in replicating his efforts. He created sample scripts to show me how I could begin and end each episode, and though I edited his drafts to make the voice my own, those scripts were enormously valuable because they gave me something to react to.

After I recorded my guest interviews, Knox edited the show to my specifications and created the final version of each episode. The first two episodes took serious work, but after that I was able to streamline my workflow, reserving my focus for creating the show, and let Knox focus on producing it.

Outsourcing the technical aspects of podcasting freed me up to focus on the things I was best at, the things only I could do, like researching books to discuss, finding potential guests, and preparing excellent interview questions, in addition to my other work. With the help of a good team, I could see more projects through to completion, projects I wouldn't have had the capacity to take on if I were working solo.

It's Not All Up to You

Most of us intuitively understand we don't need to do every-thing ourselves, so we outsource in different ways, for different reasons. You may not think of yourself as a "delegator," per se, but you almost certainly are. Maybe you don't think twice when the air conditioner starts making funny noises; you pick up the phone and call your favorite service company. Maybe you don't want to think so hard about what's for dinner each night, so you rely on a meal-planning service or a weekly plan on a blog or in a magazine. Maybe you swear by a cleaning schedule from Pinterest so you no longer need to think about when to change the sheets or how often to clean out the fridge—you just do what the checklist says.

When we outsource these tasks—and their corresponding decisions—we may save time, we may save money, we may get a better outcome, but most pertinent to overthinking, we save our mental processing power.

Deciding What to Outsource

Strategic outsourcing helps us deal with the onslaught of decisions that come at us every day. There's always so much to decide, and it's easy for the cumulative effect to become overwhelming. (And we know from chapter 3 that feeling overwhelmed is a sure sign of decision fatigue.) It can be liberating to realize you don't have to manage everything yourself, nor do you have to make all those decisions. Looking to other sources lightens the mental load.

Different people will outsource different things, for different reasons. You won't find hard-and-fast rules here for what to consider taking off your plate. There's no one-size-fits-all checklist, because we all have different talents, interests, skill sets, and resources. But you can ask yourself the following questions when considering what to take off *your* plate.

Am I Able to Do It?

The simplest question to answer is this: Are you able to do it? If you can't do it yourself, of course it makes sense to get help— whether that's from a friend or a professional. Depending on your situation and your skill set, this might mean getting help with tutoring in math, painting a high ceiling, or putting on makeup for a media appearance.

(Sometimes we might suspect we *could* take on the project but find the idea so daunting that we *feel* like we can't. More on that in a minute.)

What if you're not able to do it right now but like the idea of learning how? Read on.

Do I Want to Do It?

When my friend Meg started her podcast, she didn't know anything about audio production—but she was highly motivated to learn. She wanted to retain total control over the listening experience she was creating for her audience, which meant being hands-on with each episode, from start to finish. But her decision to do it herself was also driven by a deeper purpose. She told me that when she first began the show, "I was coming out of a dark season of postpartum depression, and the choice to allow myself to be a beginner, to learn some new skills, and to see a thing through from idea to end product brought some major healing and joy to my life on a personal level." She didn't know how to edit her own audio, but it was important to her that she learn.

Starting a podcast is a big project, but the same principles apply to everyday decisions. The bakery makes perfectly good muffins, but is baking your favorite form of stress relief? The neighbor's kid could cut the grass, but do you find the experience pleasantly meditative and the results pleasingly tangible? Your neighbor offers to return your library books, but do you enjoy stopping in to check the new-release shelf and greet your favorite librarians? Your friend adores her meal-planning service, but do you enjoy getting out your cookbooks and planning a week's worth of better-than-basic menus and a shopping list to match? You could call the plumber, but would you rather watch a few YouTube videos and fix the leak yourself? Whether you do the work yourself to save sixty dollars or for the satisfaction of a job well done, the results could be worth it.

What do you want to do yourself? The answers to this question are variable and individual, and the reasons you do or don't outsource may not be readily apparent to others. That's all okay.

Would It Be Meaningful to Do It Myself?

When deciding what to have someone else do, the question is, What is important to you? A task that needs doing is not the same thing as a task that needs to be done by *you*.

A travel pro once told me that when you're traveling for work, you shouldn't waste your mental energy figuring out transportation logistics, like negotiating public transit in an unfamiliar city. Just get a taxi and be done with it—because now it's the driver's job to figure out where you're going, and you can save your mental energy for your important meetings and presentations. That makes sense if you're in town for a high-stakes meeting (a rare occasion for me). However, we've taken our kids to New York City a few times, and with them, public transit is part of the adventure. It takes loads of mental energy to figure it out, but that's okay, because the process is part of the experience.

My friend Ashley is currently spending hours and hours planning a literary road trip for the coming autumn. Is she spending way more mental energy on this than necessary? Absolutely. If she wanted to save time, she could download somebody else's sample itinerary from the internet. But for Ashley, planning is a delightful, not-to-be-missed part of the process. It's part of the travel experience, and she loves every part of the experience.

Don't outsource something that feels important for you to do yourself. If you draw meaning from researching every aspect of your travel experience, ordering lunch for a friend, or choosing a card for a loved one, go right ahead. It's not overthinking if you're giving it the amount of thought you want to.

Can I Afford to Do It?

When we talk about being able to afford things, we tend to think of money first—and when it comes to outsourcing, money is certainly a factor. We might like the sound of outsourcing Oprah-style, hiring a personal chef, trainer, housekeeper, and who knows what else. But even if we wanted to, the cost would be prohibitive for most of us. Outsourcing doesn't always require money, but when it does, it's an important factor to consider.

Since we're talking about protecting our headspace, let's also consider this question from a different angle. Ask yourself, Can I afford the mental space to handle the thing myself? Do I have room in my brain and my life to take it on? You can only do so much.

When the answer is no, it's time to outsource.

Deciding Who to Outsource To

When it comes to getting help, sometimes the right person for the job is obvious. Sometimes it's less so. We all have different areas of expertise, and there are people in our lives who possess skills and resources we lack.

You can lighten your mental load by getting someone else to do a certain task, but for you to relax and feel like the matter is truly off your plate, you need to trust them to do the job. Otherwise, you'll still be thinking about it, which defeats the purpose. Here are some things to consider when you're trying to decide who to outsource to.

Is This the Right Person for the Job?

While you don't need to be 100 percent confident to move forward, spend a moment considering if you have good reason to outsource to a specific person. (To those who do this automatically, I salute you. To those who tend to learn these things the hard way, read on.)

Years ago, I hired someone to paint the exterior of my potentially cute but run-down first home. I was young, with no experience in these matters, and I didn't know what colors to choose. So I asked my painter to decide. "I'll tell you what *I* like," he said, and he described the color scheme he'd choose for *his* dream house. Grateful for an answer, I told him that would be just fine—and he painted the house accordingly.

The painter was skilled, but I was never satisfied with the way the paint job turned out, and it wasn't till years later that I realized why. I had been eager to outsource the color decision, but if I'd been listening, I would have realized that the painter and I had different tastes. I would have been happier with the result if I had gotten help from someone whose taste better matched my own.

Now I ask myself, *Is getting this kind of help from this particular person likely to generate the result I'm hoping for?* It's a simple question, but an important one.

Might I Ask a Friend for Help?

Asking for help doesn't have to be a formal affair; it's probably part of your life already. If you've ever called in a friend to help with a move or a closet cleanout or an outfit choice, you know what I'm talking about. When we observe our friends' skills and talents, it's obvious how much they could help us, if we asked. We'd be thrilled to get their help, and we know we'd appreciate the result.

When I reorganized my home office, I was overwhelmed by the sheer number of papers that needed filing and sorting, and I didn't know how to implement a good system for storing them. After fretting about the situation for too long, I finally asked my organized friend Melissa for tips to deal with the rapidly accumulating paperwork. Seeing I was stuck, Melissa took over. She showed up with her favorite hanging folders and Sharpies, demonstrated exactly what to do, and saved me so much mental energy (not to mention time). And it was *fun*. I was hesitant to involve someone else in my tiresome project, but Melissa was happy to help. And when we did it together, it wasn't boring.

My friend Myquillyn has an outsourcing rule of thumb that makes it possible for her to have people over without losing her mind. She loves to have company but knows from experience that if she tries to do all the cooking herself, she ends up distracted and scattered, regretting having issued the invitations. She long ago decided that when she has people over, she makes only two things—and either buys the rest or has her guests bring them.

When I stayed at her house, I saw this in action. For a cozy dinner in, Myquillyn made chicken tortellini soup at the kitchen counter, a recipe she said she'd made a hundred times, while we all hung out in the kitchen. She paired it with store-bought bread and dessert. It was delicious and easy, she was fully present, and no one felt cheated of anything—including her company. Her personal guideline lets her focus on the aspect of entertaining she likes most, the thing only *she* can do: enjoy the company of her friends.

Myquillyn has also found that people like to help. We tend to forget that when we ask for help, the benefit is twofold. We may worry that we're burdening our friends with our problems, but they want to be valuable too. Give people space to do what they do best, and besides, asking for help also gives you an excuse to see your friends a little more.

Sometimes You Need a Pro

Sometimes our friends are the professionals, which is fun, but sometimes we would benefit from hiring someone else to get the job done. We can save ourselves loads of mental energy when we rely on someone else's expertise.

When my girls were little, I wanted to paint my daughters' room. My husband and I had previously slept in that bedroom, and when we did, the walls were khaki-colored ("Sea Sand," according to Porter Paints), but now I wanted a pale lavender for the girls to coordinate with their new bedspread. I thought about asking for help but talked myself out of it. *It's just paint*, I thought. *I can handle a little paint.*

I pored over paint swatches, made some decisions, and tried a few samples on the wall. But I kept getting the color wrong. My first try looked like grape soda, so I studied magazines and more paint swatches and tried again. My second attempt looked like cough medicine; the third shade looked more pink than purple. I gave up in frustration and made an appointment with the designer at the paint store down the street, the one with impeccable taste who has recommended a half dozen colors I've loved in the past, and she does it for free. I brought her my swatches and the bedspread. "Don't feel bad," she said, "purple is hard." And then she instantly identified a shade I never would have selected but looked perfect on the wall. My girls loved it, and so did I.

That was the last time I tried to pick my own paint color. Now I let a pro pick my colors for me—and they look great, on the first try, every time.

It's worth noting that though I don't enjoy the process, others do. When my teenage daughter redecorated her room last year, she wanted to choose a new wall color herself; she saw it as a not-to-be-missed part of the experience of making her space her own. With my help, she first browsed Pinterest, then visited Home Depot, then painted a few swatches on the wall. It was a long process, and in this situation, that was okay.

Deciding When to Outsource

Sometimes life puts us in situations where we could benefit from a little more (or a lot more) outside support than we typically need; sometimes we need help at specific *stages* of a project.

Remember That Life Is Lived in Seasons

Some seasons of life are predictably stressful—moving to a new home, tackling a busy time at work, having a baby, or surviving fall sports season. Some days and seasons require us to be more strategic than others about what we get someone else to do. There's a reason we take soup to the sick, help our friends move, and are tempted by takeout when deadlines loom.

We can approach outsourcing with a spirit of experimentation by trying different things for different seasons, seeing how it works out, and then incorporating what we've learned when it's time to move forward.

When You Need Help Getting Started

We can save vast amounts of mental energy by asking for help at the beginning of a project. Once we're in motion, it's easy to stay in motion, but it can take a whole lot of effort to get started.

Have you experienced the daunting feeling of needing to begin? I'm a writer, and I know too well how overwhelming a blank page can be. It's hard work to turn *nothing* into *something*. But once I have a draft—even a shoddy one—I can make it better.

If the idea of starting something is daunting, think about how you could get someone else to help you create a metaphorical first draft. Can someone else create the starting point?

Just yesterday at the coffee shop, I happened to sit next to two women who were deep in conversation and I couldn't help overhearing. One had just been diagnosed with celiac disease, an autoimmune disorder that requires the scrupulous elimination of gluten from the diet. She was overwhelmed by the complexity of the task before her—learning a new way to shop, eat, and cook— and asked her friend, who had a family member with celiac, to walk her through everything she needed to know.

I heard them discuss the learning curve for a strict gluten-free lifestyle. "I open the fridge and have no idea what to do next," the recently diagnosed woman said.

"It feels overwhelming at first," her friend told her, "but you'll get the hang of it. This is what I wish I'd known when we got started." She then pulled out a file folder full of articles, spreadsheets, and grocery lists. They discussed go-to recipes for meals and snacks, strategies for eating out, and what to do when she got "glutened" accidentally. When one woman had no idea where to start, her experienced friend showed her the way.

Similarly, readers tell me they love the annual *Modern Mrs Darcy* Reading Challenge because they don't need to draw on their own creative energy to get started. We give them a starting point by establishing a structure for them to work within. People tweak the challenge for their own use, but we give them the first draft.

I've learned to implement this principle in the workplace as well. Starting things is hard, and there's no need for me to make every decision myself. My small team is smart and talented, with lots to contribute. So when we begin projects, I often ask them to give me a starting point by brainstorming ideas, sending me tasks they're willing and able to take on, and proposing time frames and deadlines. It's much easier to react to something they've already started than it is to create something from whole cloth myself. I'll ask for clarification and provide feedback, but I don't generate the first draft on my own. You may not manage a team, but the principle is transferable: When you're getting started, can someone else give you something to respond to?

When You Need Help Wrapping Up Loose Ends

Insecurity and fear generate a tremendous amount of over-thinking about matters big and small. When we're not sure we're doing it right, whatever *it* is, we can't mentally move on, so we un-intentionally leave the door open to overthinking. When we lack confidence in our own judgment, it's natural—even, in a perverse way, useful—for our thoughts to repeatedly return to unanswered questions or unresolved situations, because our brains don't like unfinished business. If we can get someone we trust to tell us to rest easy, we can stop this pernicious thought cycle.

Some situations in life are never going to be 100 percent re-solved, so why not strive to preserve your mental energy by resolving the things you can? This can be as simple as getting a pro to confirm you're doing it right. Years ago, before CrossFit entered the mainstream, I followed their program, lifting weights at home in our garage. Relying on books and YouTube for guid-ance, I taught myself moves like "snatch" and "sumo deadlift"—exercises in which proper form is crucial, both for efficacy and safety. I thought my form was okay, but I was far from sure—and every time I worked out, I wondered if I was doing it right.

A year into my CrossFit journey, work took me to Chicago, a city that, at the time, was home to one of the country's few Cross-Fit gyms. I made an appointment to visit and specifically asked for help assessing my form on foundational weightlifting moves. Lifting with an audience felt strange—I'd learned the moves on YouTube, and another human had never seen me execute them—but it was worth it. The coach's simple words—"you're doing it right"—stopped my overthinking immediately.

I've found that sometimes a simple conversation can resolve years of persistent worry over recurring themes like these: *Am I supporting my daughter's schoolwork in the way she needs?* (The school counselor confirms that she's doing just fine and doesn't need or want you to become a helicopter parent. *You're doing it right.*) *Am I killing my fiddle leaf fig with overwatering?* (The whiz at the local plant shop confirms that, nope, despite what the internet says, because of our climate here, *you're doing it right.*) *I've just been putting moisturizer on that irritated skin, but is it a symptom of something more serious?* (The doctor confirms that's exactly what you need to do and there's nothing to worry about, *you're doing it right.*)

It's easy to miss the potential here for outsourcing, because we're not necessarily outsourcing an item on our to-do list. We're enlisting someone else's help to answer a lingering question. And once that decision is made, it no longer takes up space in our mind. When you know you're doing it right, your brain can rest easy. You don't feel compelled to wonder about that issue anymore, because that thought loop is closed.

Ask for Help and Live Your Best Life

We don't have to do it all ourselves. When we get someone else to do it, we give ourselves the gift of one less thing to worry about, one less thing to handle, one less thing to manage so we can put our mental energy to better use. And that's just one thing; imagine the cumulative effect of doing this repeatedly!

This strategy safeguards our mental space and often carries fun bonuses besides. We save time, we have fun with friends, we may even save money. We get smarter thanks to the expertise of others, and we learn things we didn't even know we didn't know.

Getting someone else to do it isn't just a savvy strategy. It's a way to do our best work and live our best lives.

Don't be shy. Ask for help.

············· Next Steps ·············

1. Can you think of an outsourcing success story, a time when you sought out needed help with a project and were happy with the results? What was it?

....

....

....

....

2. What is something you wouldn't want to outsource, even if you could, because you enjoy it so much?

....

....

....

....

3. What is something you've been struggling with that you can ask for help with? Who can you ask to help?

....

....

....

....

4. When have you experienced a season where you needed to outsource more than usual? Do you anticipate living through a busy season in the coming months? What might you outsource to help you through it?

....

....

....

....

5. Is there an area in your life where you wonder if you're doing it right? How might you be able to get help tying up those loose ends?

....

....

....

....

Part 3

Let the Sun Shine In

10

When Things Go
Sideways

*Why not seize the pleasure at once? How often is happiness
destroyed by preparation, foolish preparation!*

Jane Austen

During my senior year of college, the whole campus lost
power for one day. My first clue was when I arrived at the
library for my 8:00 a.m. shift to reshelve returned books before
class. I tugged on the door, surprised to find it locked and the
interior eerily dark. Only then did I notice the sign: power was
out campus wide, academic and administrative buildings were
closed, all classes were canceled.

I hurried home to share the news with my roommates. We
cheered our good fortune, and those who weren't already dressed
didn't hurry to change out of their pajamas. We had the whole

day in front of us, and it was blissfully, unexpectedly open. No one had had an opportunity to make plans for the day—how could we have? We didn't know it would happen. This was the '90s; nobody owned cell phones that beeped with text alerts while we were sleeping.

The timing was exceptional. It happened to be a gorgeous spring day, warm and sunny. Everyone headed outside to the quad, where they studied or played Frisbee or chatted with friends. The campus looked like the cover of a college brochure. Picnic-style meals were served out on the sidewalk, and instead of dining indoors at the usual cafeteria tables, we ate outdoors on the cool grass.

It was a wonderful day, the kind you couldn't have planned if you wanted to, and one I still remember fondly. And it started with something going all wrong.

Some of us seek opportunities to be spontaneous and go off script, while some of us have a plan for every minute of our day. But whether we're "go with the flow" by nature or prefer a carefully crafted routine, life can force us to improvise. Things beyond our control inevitably happen—the sitter cancels, the rain necessitates a change of plans, the power goes out—and we have to pivot in the moment, making the best of the situation. We have to change course, and we have to do it fast.

These moments when things go sideways often feel like something we have to survive. Any kind of time-sensitive situation—where we have to make a choice *right now*—is ripe for overthinking and decision paralysis.

We can't prepare for every situation, but we can plan for things going awry, as they certainly will. We can create a framework that allows for spontaneity—thus inviting good stuff into our lives—because things don't always turn out as we intend. And we can take comfort in this: spontaneous moments can also lead to some of the best memories, like that glorious spring day when my college classes were canceled. An unexpected turn of events may throw us into momentary disarray, but if we can push through the messy middle of renegotiating our decisions in a hurry, we may find joy on the other side. The trick is knowing how to get there. Let's explore how we can do just that.

Just Pick Something

When it comes to overthinking, any opportunity for decision-making is fraught with peril, *especially* when time is of the essence. Even choosing between good options is tough, and the added time pressure raises the stakes. It's easy to feel overwhelmed in the moment and to choose poorly because of it.

I've done this myself, sadly, on numerous occasions. Once when Will and I were in Manhattan, we'd carefully planned our itinerary in advance so we could spend our trip *enjoying* New York instead of *deciding* what to do. One day we planned to spend an hour at the Museum of Modern Art and the next wandering north toward Central Park. But when we walked out of the museum at closing time, we were surprised to face an unexpected downpour. This wasn't walking weather, not for unprepared tourists like us. But we had a whole hour until our next scheduled event nearby—and so we were forced to be spontaneous. Instead of taking a stroll, we thought, *Why not duck into a little shop or restaurant for a cup of coffee?*

But we had no idea where to go; we weren't familiar with this part of town. We hadn't planned ahead, we didn't have any recommendations to rely on, and none of the places nearby looked promising. We didn't want to stand on the street corner googling our options; besides, we didn't have time for that. But we also didn't want to end up someplace lousy, wasting time and money on something that wasn't any good. We kept cycling through the same options—the lackluster-looking places we could see on the block and the better ones we knew about that were a bit too far away—but none of them seemed inviting. We were afraid of choosing poorly, and we froze. We didn't choose *anything*. We couldn't decide, so we, in effect, decided to do nothing and were stuck walking in the rain.

This was not a high-stakes situation, and the consequences weren't serious. It was just a little rain, an afternoon drink. But it illustrates how otherwise reasonable people can completely seize up, unable to successfully cope with a small change of plans. This situation is all too common. We're afraid of choosing poorly, so we end up choosing nothing—not because it was the right decision, but because we couldn't get through the messy middle. We couldn't move past our overthinking and take action. "Not being able to decide" is a lousy reason not to do something fun, yet it happens every day. When we're unsure what to do, or feeling tired or overwhelmed, we default to the status quo . . . which means we do nothing.

The consequences may not have been serious that time, but that won't always be the case. We need to learn to do better.

I have a friend who is a self-professed expert on dipping into bars and restaurants for a drink and a snack. When she travels, she finds great places all over the country to stop and grab a drink or a bite to eat. After my own disappointing experience in New York, I asked her how she chooses where to go on the fly. What's her secret?

"I do this all the time," she said, "so it's second nature now." She explained that while she's found a ton of great places on short notice, she's also visited some real duds. But she's up for trying just about anything.

"You want my secret?" she asked. "The worst that can happen isn't that bad. So I just pick something."

When it's clear a decision is needed to move forward, the worst thing we can do is not act. Making a choice—any choice—is better than staying stuck debating our options, letting the moment pass us by. The next time you face this kind of decision, try adopting my friend's mindset. Just pick something, anything. It's better than doing nothing, and besides, things that don't unfold according to plan often make the best memories. So what if, instead of resisting these sideways moments, we leaned into the decision, knowing that good things may await us on the other side?

Lean In, Expecting Good Things

Our perspective impacts how well we deal with the situation at hand. When we perceive the stakes to be high, we're more likely to freeze—especially if we're prone to perfectionism. When spontaneity strikes (ha!), it's helpful to purposefully adopt a low-stakes mindset. Instead of striving to choose the ideal option, we can aim to choose a good one, reminding ourselves that the best memories often start with something going wrong. And then, instead of resisting the change of plans, we can lean in, expecting good things. As a bonus, this lowers our anxiety, which makes it easier to decide.

When the power went out at my college, we didn't feel pressured to maximize our one precious day off. We didn't stay indoors and debate our options for hours, because we felt like there was no way we could screw it up. Ironically, when we feel pressured to spend our time well, it can be harder to do so. We felt no pressure, and so we leaned into the strangeness of the day, expecting good things—and we found them.

A few years ago, Will and I had another New York experience, similar to the one I told you about, but this time we handled the sideways moment much better. It was the last morning of a fun and productive business trip. We had only a few more hours in town; our bags were already packed and waiting with the bellhop so we could explore unencumbered before heading to the airport for our 2:00 p.m. flight. We were standing at the 9/11 memorial when our phones chirped with identical texts: our flight had been canceled, no more flights were available that day, and we'd already been rebooked to fly out the next morning. Will and I suddenly found ourselves with an extra eighteen hours in New York.

We wouldn't have wished for this to happen; we'd planned to come home when we did for good reason. But after surveying our options and confirming that we were indeed "stuck" in the city for another night, we relished the possibilities. What could we do with that time?

We'd carefully planned every minute of the previous days in town, but now, faced with eighteen open hours, we didn't panic about how "best" to spend them. It all looked like bonus time, and we were up for anything. (At least we were once we confirmed our kids at home could stay with my mom another night and we could check right back into our same hotel.) We didn't have a careful plan, because how could we? We hadn't expected to still be around, but since we were, we'd put that time to good use. We felt like there was no way we could screw it up.

We weren't striving to do memorable things; the situation itself was memorable enough. We went to a museum we hadn't had time for, ate at a neighborhood spot that looked promising, and walked miles and miles.

While Will and I didn't choose for our flight to be canceled, other times it's our own mistakes that take us off script. Take this example from my friend Bill.

He and his wife, Sheila, enjoy touring wineries when they travel and often purchase bottles of wine to bring home as souvenirs. One ordinary Tuesday, Sheila opened a bottle of wine to go with their dinner. She poured two glasses and took a sip, saying, "This is really good." Bill took a sip and concurred. It was *incredibly* good. He took a close look at the label to see what they were drinking, and that's when he realized their mistake—they'd inadvertently opened an eighty-dollar bottle they'd been saving for a special occasion! They could have kicked themselves for the mix-up, but instead of indulging regret, they decided to lean into their "mistake." Their ordinary Tuesday evening turned into the special occasion they'd been waiting for. They got out the cloth napkins, lit candles, and lingered over dinner, talking about the wineries they'd visited in the past and those they hoped to visit in the future. From those visits, they'd bring home more souvenir bottles, bottles that could be the makings of future special, ordinary nights.

I'm reminded of a scene from the Alexander Payne movie *Sideways*, in which Miles confesses to his friend Maya that he hasn't yet opened a '61 Cheval Blanc because he's been waiting for a special occasion, even though he's already had it so long it is in danger of going bad. Maya encourages him, saying, "The day you open a '61 Cheval Blanc, that's the special occasion."

Build In Margin for the Unexpected

Sometimes spontaneity is thrust upon us, but what about those times when we have a choice of whether to veer off script? When we are *invited* rather than *forced* to be spontaneous? I've found it's much easier to lean into those moments if I make space in my life for the unexpected.

When we're operating at 100 percent capacity, we're unable to deviate from our plans. We don't have the margin. But by making space in our schedules—that is, by not maintaining lives and calendars that are jammed to capacity—we are better able to improvise. One of the ways I do this is by planning to meet my deadlines early, knowing full well that things go wrong and schedules get disrupted. Someone gets the flu, the internet goes out, the space bar on my laptop quits working at exactly the wrong moment. (Yes, that really happened.)

When we're prepared, we're available to seize opportunities as they present themselves, whether they are thrust upon us or we invite them in. Sometimes plans get thrown off and we have to recalibrate, as we've already discussed—but sometimes an opportunity appears where we weren't expecting it.

When we build in margin, we're not just preparing for things to go wrong. We're also preparing for things to go unexpectedly *right*. When I was young, my mom always told me to do my homework early so that if I wanted to play with a friend, I'd be able to. I wouldn't be stuck at home rushing to finish my homework. Now that I'm an adult, this advice continues to be true—even if the details now look a little different.

When we're prepared, we can take advantage of opportunities as they arise. It's one thing to tell yourself that you value your personal relationships, but it's another to make space in your schedule to live this out. For example: If I'm dropping something off at a friend's house and she invites me to stay for a cup of tea, sometimes the answer has to be no. But if I make a habit of building margin into my days, I can say yes without panicking about getting through my to-do list. I can take the time to sit and have a nice conversation instead of rushing out the door.

When we have wiggle room in our schedules, we can choose to be there in the moments life presents us with. Sometimes these take us by surprise, but sometimes we can see them coming, like last year when we were eagerly awaiting news on our friend's tenure application. After a lengthy process, we knew he was supposed to find out any day. On the day Will and I heard the good news, we took another look at our to-do lists, saw we had margin, and ran to the wine shop for a bottle of champagne. We dropped it off at his house right then, in the middle of the day, and got to congratulate him in person. We couldn't have done this if we hadn't made a practice of building leeway into our schedules.

Not being in survival mode means it's not such a production to embrace spontaneity. This is the same reason we build in extra time in case someone gets the flu right before a big deadline, but it's the fun version.

If your house is tidy enough, you can be hospitable (or you could just be ready to pile everything in the laundry basket to clean up). If your chores are done (or at least not terribly overdue), you're free to do something fun with friends when the prospect presents itself. Our family has gotten better about deliberately embracing these spontaneous opportunities, like bumping into friends and inviting them to come back to our house for lunch. When the fridge is stocked and the work is more or less done, it opens up room to bring more unplanned joy into our lives.

Because it's different, breaking from routine can be especially memorable. So lean in. Maybe you glimpse the makings of a lovely sunset, so you take a walk to get a good look. Maybe the weather is exceptionally brilliant, so you scrap your Saturday chores and head to the park. (On a beautiful and unseasonably warm day, it often seems like the whole city is at the park, for exactly this reason.) In these instances, you may need to remind yourself that the status quo is always the easier path. But staying home isn't memorable—there's a reason to take action!

Take Advantage of These Opportunities

You may not rejoice when your plan goes awry or your routine is disrupted; many overthinkers innately cling to structure and predictability. Consider that your routines and plans—when you build in margin—create space for spontaneity.

When faced with an unexpected moment of decision, it's easy to freeze. But to get to the other side where the good stuff is, you have to enter into the messy middle of uncertainty and decision. The joy is at the end, and the only way out is through.

Sure, this can be hard. When you're forced to pivot, you have to decide, and maybe you don't want to. It's easier to go with the path of least resistance. But there are reasons for being smart about spontaneity. Don't waste those opportunities; take advantage of them.

·············· Next Steps ··············

1. How do you typically react when things change unexpectedly?

   ....

   ....

   ....

   ....

2. What's the last spontaneous thing you did? How did it turn out?

   ....

   ....

   ....

   ....

3. Have you ever experienced a special moment because of a "mistake"? What was it?

   ....

   ....

   ....

   ....

4. When have you successfully managed to "just pick something"?

....

....

....

....

5. Do you feel like you currently have margin in your life for the unexpected? If yes, what is working? If no, how can you build in that margin?

....

....

....

....

11

Rituals to Rely On

Rituals, Al decided, were a lot like numbers; they offered comforting solidity in the otherwise chaotic floodtide of life. But it was more than that. A ritual was a way to hold time— not freezing it, rather the opposite, warming it through the touch of your imagination.

Erica Bauermeister

How many of us begin our days with morning coffee? You might pour coffee into your travel mug as you rush out the door, downing the caffeine as you head to work or the gym or the bus stop. But imagine that you adopt a new practice. Maybe you decide you'll carve out a moment to savor the first sips. Perhaps you'll resolve to name a few things you're thankful for and set simple intentions for the day to come while you drink. The first option is routine, but for the second, the ritual is as important as the beverage.

Imagine the scene unfolding like this. Your morning begins exactly like millions of other people's: you stagger out of bed and head straight for the kitchen.

You used to have to wait for the water in the kettle to come to a boil on the stove, but you finally purchased that electric kettle you'd been eyeing, the programmable one that has the water hot and ready when you wake up. On cold mornings like this, it's your strongest motivation for getting out of bed, because you know that first cup of coffee is just minutes away.

You get out the scale, measure the beans, and tip them into the grinder. The noise hits your ears first, then the aroma of freshly ground coffee fills the kitchen. You tap the freshly ground beans into the filter and begin to pour, watching the scale creep toward the 350 grams that will fill your cup. You like to hit the magic number right on the nose.

You used to steal a few minutes to read while you poured the water, but you don't do that anymore. You've learned that, at least for this first cup, you like to focus on what's happening here, now, before the day takes on a life of its own. And so you pour in rhythmic circles, watching the coffee bloom in the filter, listening to it trickle into your cup, observing how the smell changes and blossoms.

You tend to rotate among a few mugs, but this morning you grab your favorite one, clean and waiting for you in the cabinet. You pour your brew, enjoying the sound of it sloshing into your mug.

You sit down in your chair with your freshly poured cup, your journal, and your morning reading. You savor the first sips, thankful for the gift of good coffee, then pick up your book. You're currently making your way through a Parker Palmer title. You have only a few chapters to go; you idly wonder what you'll read next. Maybe one of those poetry collections you keep buying but not reading? A few poems a morning could be just the thing to set the tone for the day. But now is not the time to think about that, so you brush the thought away and pick up the Palmer book.

The chapter is short, so you read another. You have time. Right now it feels like you've got nothing but time. When your coffee's half gone, you reach for your journal and take a look at today's to-do list, the one you made last night. Now that you're awake and feeling centered, you're ready to see what the day holds.

You can begin your day with a cup of coffee. Or you can take your daily routine and turn it into a ritual, one that invites you to remember who you are, what you value, and what you want to accomplish.

How Routines Can Become Rituals

At first blush, rituals and routines have much in common. The difference between the two is not necessarily the action but the attitude behind it. A routine is done for expediency. But *ritual* derives from a Latin word that describes things pertaining to religious rites, a connotation still in use today. The word can also refer to something a person does habitually and constantly, almost religiously. Ritual is something we do with a higher purpose in mind.

How we think about things changes the way we experience them. This is true for rituals—we don't need a ceremony or special occasion to experience their power and pleasure. Rituals can be done regularly, built around small things. That morning coffee is habitual (routine), but it can also be made meaningful (ritual)—and I'm not just talking about the caffeine.

It doesn't have to be difficult to elevate a routine so it becomes a ritual. You could regularly call your sister on weekend mornings. Or you could call her on purpose, setting early Saturday aside as a time to curl up in your favorite chair, phone in hand, and share not only what's on your mind that morning but also the highlights of the week gone by, your hopes for the week to come, and your concerns about your parents, your kids, your job. One is routine; the other is ritual.

You might routinely order pizza on Friday nights because you're exhausted after a hard week and can't handle thinking about dinner. Or Friday pizza night could be a ritual. When the workweek is over, you welcome the weekend by cranking up some music, uncorking a bottle of wine, lovingly rolling out the dough, and then tossing a salad while the pizza bakes. Soon you're ready to sit down and enjoy your homemade meal, as is your Friday-night custom. You could also lovingly order Domino's; it's something we've often done at my house with a fervent spirit of gratitude. It's not the pizza that makes it a ritual, it's the attitude behind it.

Elevating something to ritual status doesn't require much; it's all in the way you approach it. When my friend left sunny Arizona for snowy Utah, her family struggled to adjust to the new-to-them winter climate. So they decided that every year, they'd take a trip to someplace warm. And they did one more significant thing. To remind everyone of the purpose behind the trip, they gave it a name: the Winter Escape Trip. This simple act made the trip feel more purposeful and important. The name reminded everyone why they were going, why they needed it, what it meant to them, and what it said about who they are as a family. The name changed the way they thought about the trip—and about themselves.

While consistency is key, the form the ritual takes may vary. Your rituals may change with the seasons, whether that's the season of the year or the season of life. An early morning run by the water may be torture in winter's cold but essential in July's heat. As the seasons change, a restorative afternoon cup of tea could become a restorative afternoon cup of iced-something. We can rely on the ritual while adapting the particulars as needed.

The Power of Ritual

There's no one-size-fits-all approach to ritual. The same ritual that serves your friend well may be the last thing you're interested in doing, and that's fine. The power of ritual is not in the morning coffee or the Friday pizza or the four "lucky" taps a batter gives home plate before the pitch but in *the ritual itself.* Generally speaking, it matters little what the ritual is. A ritual—any ritual—establishes a certain kind of mindset; perhaps this is why rituals benefit even those who claim they're not important. When a routine works for us, we don't have to pay attention to it, but a ritual calls us to fully participate in what we're doing—even if it's as simple as savoring a cup of tea. The specific action doesn't matter, but its rhythm, regularity, and meaning do. We enter into our life purposefully when we do it with ritual, meeting each experience fresh but also with a rhythm that supports us.

Rituals Help Us Practice Mindfulness

While we can mindlessly follow a routine, we cannot do the same with a ritual. A ritual unites the rhythm of routine with focused attention—a powerful combination for avoiding overthinking. It's hard to overthink when we are focused on the moment. The ritual also forces us to *slow down*—and when we deliberately slow our bodies, we slow our minds as well.

What we're thinking about during our ritual isn't important. What's important is all the things we're *not* thinking about. Our minds are focused on what's right in front of us. Will we wander off the path as the day goes on? Sure we will. But we'll wander a lot less if we establish the right direction.

The right morning ritual encourages us to approach our day with intention. If we begin by purposefully drinking coffee, practicing gratitude, and journaling, we will conclude that time feeling calm, centered, and ready to take on the day with the big picture in mind. This early morning ritual frames the day and focuses the mind, two valuable practices for those who wish to avoid overthinking. We won't feel rushed or harried. We'll be present. When we don't intentionally set our focus, our minds wander wherever they want—and that can be scary business.

A word of caution. It is possible to inadvertently adopt a ritual that focuses your attention on the wrong things, fueling over-thinking. Perhaps your morning ritual involves browsing news sites while you drink your morning coffee. Your intentions are good—you value being an informed citizen and want to begin the day knowledgeable about current events. But instead of feeling focused on your priorities, you feel info-bombed and spend the rest of the morning fretting about the headlines.

If your morning ritual sends you into the day feeling stressed and scattered, choose quiet reading material instead, something that puts you in the right headspace. What you choose to focus on matters. Your morning ritual sets the tone for the whole day, so avoid rituals that set you up for overthinking, thus robbing you of the meaning and peace rituals can bring.

Rituals Help Us Reset

As our minds inevitably wander throughout the day, our rituals can gently nudge our thoughts back to where they belong. For many years, I religiously followed a 2:00 p.m. ritual. Whenever I mentioned my unusual midday break, people were intrigued and quizzed me for details.

Back then I spent the mornings working as fast as I could. My mental and physical energy would predictably fade in the early afternoon, and by two o'clock I was toast.

I'd turn off my computer, make a cup of coffee, grab a book, and read for fifteen minutes. This brief indulgence provided a sense of balance and control, even if my day so far had felt unbalanced and out of control. Next, I'd spend a few minutes reviewing my to-do list for the rest of the day and reset my priorities before getting back to work.

This ritual served as a stop sign, a fail-safe, an island of respite free from overthinking where, in a sense, I got to start over. No matter how far off track my mind had wandered, at 2:00 p.m. I hit the reset button. By the time I wrapped up my midday break— which I could get through in just twenty minutes if I had to—I felt refreshed and ready to purposefully take on the rest of the day. And while I most enjoyed this ritual when I was actually reading, it helped me in the morning too. If I was tired or harried, knowing that a 2:00 p.m. reset was on the horizon was good for morale.

Because I once blogged about my 2:00 p.m. ritual, many readers have written over the years to tell me about the afternoon rituals they were subsequently inspired to implement. The pattern has been striking. Based on my readers' responses, an effective midday reset should include a little bit of pleasure (like my coffee and reading), a little bit of prioritizing, and a little bit of perambulating (a number of readers swore by a quick walk or run or other time in the fresh air).

If you want to establish your own rituals but aren't sure where to begin, know that these elements have served your fellow readers well. Again, it doesn't much matter what the ritual is, only that you follow it consistently.

Evening Rituals Help Us Get Ready to Sleep

For many of us, bedtime is prime overthinking time. We lie in bed, our thoughts drifting toward the events of the day gone by, thinking of things we could have done differently and fretting about what tomorrow holds.

Bedtime is a great time to harness the power of ritual. It eases the body into a restful frame of mind so you can nod off peacefully.

As a bonus, regular, quality sleep—and enough of it—is vital for not overthinking, so you'll be better prepared to not overthink in the morning.

Some people listen to quiet music, or do stretches, or write in a journal they keep by the bed. I know what *I* like to do before bed. I begin in the kitchen, because I've found that thinking about the next morning inspires me to get to bed on time. I choose the candle I'll light in the morning and set the timer on the kettle so the water is hot when I wake up. The last thing I do is read a few chapters of an interesting novel—but not a thriller, lest I be tempted to stay up too late—before I turn out the light. I prefer fiction before bed, because instead of dwelling on my own concerns at bedtime, I focus on those of fictional characters and go to sleep thinking about *their* problems instead of my own.

Rituals Connect Us to One Another

Strong relationships are good for us, and rituals are an excellent way to build them. They can be as simple as a standing coffee date you religiously observe, a supper club with friends who consciously celebrate coming together, or a weeknight family dinner. Much research has been devoted to the family dinner, and the results are staggering: this simple ritual increases children's emotional stability; bolsters their sense of identity, self-confidence, and connectedness; and deepens their spirit of resilience—all attributes that give them a strong foundation from which to venture out into the world (or, let's face it, into the caves of their own minds). This strong foundation is particularly helpful during times of transition or increased stress.

There's nothing remarkable about the dinner hour. The important thing is what happens when we gather with others—though it's true that food motivates people to show up. In fact, my mother swears her grandmother maintained close relationships with all her grandchildren because she issued a standing invitation to her entire family for Saturday morning breakfast. If they came, she would cook. They came, and she did. Without the food, they wouldn't have been as motivated to come. (Many of her grandchildren were teenage boys at the time, and my great-grandmother said it was no coincidence she built the ritual around breakfast!) The significance came not from the food but from what happened at the table: the sense of community, the conversation, and the commitment to being together.

Our friends Dave and Amanda traveled to Israel last year and saw firsthand the Shabbat ritual practiced by Jewish people there. The whole community observes a weekly day of rest, from sundown Friday until three stars appear in the Saturday evening sky. Our friends aren't Jewish, but the Jewish family who hosted them in Israel encouraged them to try the practice back home to see if it made a difference in the way they saw the world. They tried it, and it did.

Dave and Amanda went all out for their Shabbat-inspired ritual. (When I observed as much to Amanda, she laughed. "Dave doesn't do things halfway," she said.) Their new ritual consisted of special meals, a brief reading of prayers, frequent guests, and a strict no-screen rule. Dave and Amanda invited our family to join them one Friday evening, and Dave issued the invitation months in advance. We arrived on a Friday night, bearing only a bottle of wine. Dave already had his signature chicken on the grill, the same recipe he prepared every week. We ate by candlelight, following Dave's reading of their chosen prayers, and after we ate, we lingered well into the evening on the back deck.

You don't have to go all out like Dave does to experience the benefits of ritual. Elevate a simple meal or get-together to a ritual by signaling that you value it: set the table, light a candle, place some flowers at the center, or say a word of thanks for the time you're spending with friends or family. You could go all out and do all four. But the point isn't the trappings, it's the people.

Becoming the Kind of Person Who Overthinks Less

Rituals help us stop overthinking on a daily basis, both by proactively directing our focus and, when needed, stopping overthinking in its tracks. But because the benefits of practicing rituals accumulate over time, rituals also help us stop overthinking in the long term. That's because the regular practice of ritual provides rhythm and meaning to our days and increases our sense of connectedness.

Perhaps unexpectedly, rituals also bolster our sense of identity and give us a sense of security. That's because rituals aren't just something we *do*, they're something we *choose*. Rituals deliberately support our priorities, our health, and our relationships. They make our small world a better and more peaceful place. When we're grounded and healthy, we overthink less. When we're connected to people and feel supported, we're less likely to flounder.

If you want to embrace the power of ritual, you don't need to stress about finding the perfect one. Instead, aim to incorporate more rituals into your life, beginning simply and enjoying the benefits. For they are many.

Next Steps

1. What rituals do you currently rely on?

   ....

   ....

   ....

   ....

2. Are there any rituals you'd like to implement? What are
   they?

   ....

   ....

   ....

   ....

3. Can you identify any routines you could elevate to rituals? What changes would you need to make to accomplish this?

   ....

   ....

   ....

   ....

12

Let's Splurge

"You don't ever do something just because it makes you feel good?" The assistant shrugs. "Mademoiselle, you need to spend more time in Paris."

Jojo Moyes

It couldn't have been a more gracious email that sent me into a tailspin. The message confirmed our upcoming reservation for Bogel, party of six, though *reservation* isn't exactly the right word. This restaurant sells seats like a theater would for a hot show—in other words, they're nonrefundable and sell out far in advance. Will and I had purchased ours months before; it had seemed like a good idea at the time. But when I saw in print that yes, we really paid *that* amount for *this* experience, all I could think was, *What on earth were we thinking?* Why had we spent so lavishly on one dinner for our children, who might not even be old enough to appreciate it?

Will and I had been to the Chicago restaurant once before, just the two of us, to celebrate something special. And the night had been special, memorable from the first bite to the last. The food was surprising, provocative, different. It was indeed like theater, and as we ate, we kept saying, "This place would blow our kids' minds. Wouldn't it be fun to bring them?" We mentally filed a return visit into the "maybe one day" category, and long after our meal, we continued to discuss the possibility of a return trip with all six of us.

Nearly two years after that memorable meal, we bought the tickets. Will and I had been sitting on the couch watching *Parks and Recreation* while Will tinkered on his phone, when something caught his attention. "Hey," he said, "if we really want to take everyone for dinner, we can get a table for six on Memorial Day weekend." We already had plans to rendezvous with college friends in the city that weekend; we could easily tack on an extra day and go to dinner. Wouldn't that be fun?

Those tickets would be snatched up in a matter of hours, if not minutes. If we wanted them, we had to act fast—but we'd already been thinking about it for years. We decided to go for it. Will grabbed the debit card and booked a table for six, months away.

I didn't think much about those future reservations in the following months; my mind was focused on our busy present. Then the email arrived, a simple message confirming our visit. Its purpose was to set the stage for a wonderful experience, but its arrival triggered delayed sticker shock. *What had we done?* And also, *Can we undo it?* My brain raced through the possibilities, trying to think of a way to return the unreturnable and get our money back. Could we extricate ourselves from the situation? Did I really want to?

I kept thinking about our kids—specifically, I realized we never investigated whether the restaurant even allowed children.

We assumed our kids would be pleasant and well behaved, but was I kidding myself? I googled the restaurant and saw that last year the chef berated a couple for bringing a baby to dinner when their babysitter canceled. Maybe we could call and explain our situation; maybe this was our out.

With growing alarm, Will watched me rant. "What is your deal?" he asked. Though to his credit, his actual words were gentler and his questions were good ones. "We agreed to do this," he pointed out. "We've been looking forward to it. What's changed?"

I struggled to explain. "I *am* excited," I told him. "I think it will be a great night, and our kids will remember it forever. But it costs more than I'm used to spending, and *that* feels uncomfortable. I keep wondering if we did the right thing."

An Uncharacteristic Indulgence

A splurge, by nature, is an experience beyond the normal routine of our lives. It's when we spend—often, but not always, money— freely, even extravagantly, in a way we typically don't. A splurge is in the eye of the beholder; it's an indulgence that feels extravagant to *us*.

When we talk about splurging, we're not talking about impulse purchases or spending big all the time or living beyond our means. A splurge is a strategic deployment of resources. We can splurge and be financially responsible, as long as we have the resources to pay for our splurges and principles that guide them. (We can also splurge and not spend a dime. More on that in a bit.)

I like the *idea* of splurging, but perhaps because my frugal nature was reinforced by childhood training, I have a hard time taking action. I know I'm not the only one. How can we figure out if a splurge makes sense?

Accept That Signature Experiences Are Expensive

I opened that email from the restaurant and started running the numbers according to my normal cost-benefit analysis. When I calculated the cost per hour—no, the cost per minute—of our meal, knowing all we'd have to show for it at night's end would be a photo and a keepsake menu, it didn't make sense to say yes, at least not according to the way I typically made sense of things. I was afraid we might be wasting money.

Will is also a judicious spender by nature, yet he didn't freak out when the email confirming our reservation came in.

"This makes sense. We'll have fun, and the kids are old enough to appreciate it. It'll be worth the cost," he told me. Then he remembered something. "Think about it like this: Remember when we all went to Biltmore?"

I *did* remember. The year before, I'd had a book signing in Asheville, and we decided to bring the family along for the weekend. Malaprop's Bookstore graciously scheduled my visit for peak leaf season. It was a gorgeous fall weekend, colorful and mild.

We didn't plan ahead for our weekend away—we only knew we wanted to hike, eat, and visit the bookstore. While checking into our hotel that first night, we realized we were just minutes away from Biltmore Estate, George Vanderbilt's massive Châteauesque-style residence tucked into the Blue Ridge Mountains. I'd longed to see the grounds with my own eyes ever since I read about the estate's construction in Witold Rybczynski's captivating book *A Clearing in the Distance*.

Will and I began investigating. We were so close, and we had the time. We could easily buy tickets and go. But the steep entry fee gave us pause. Our kids weren't used to visiting historic houses, and I was far from confident they'd be able to appreciate the experience. I wasn't keen on spending all that money only to feel like we wasted it. How could we decide?

In the middle of our deliberations, Will remembered an article he'd read that captured some of our unarticulated feelings. The article set forth this simple truth about the economics of travel: an area's big destinations—or "signature experiences"—often come with a big price tag, and it helps to keep that in mind when sticker shock hits. They're often expensive for good reason, and often worth it. (Unlike silly things like the six-dollar bottles of water at the zoo or terrible airport coffee—nobody calls those things *pleasantly* extravagant.) Biltmore was undoubtedly a signature experience. The price was beyond the usual for us, but the experience promised to be as well.

I value making memories, so I suppressed my reflexive cringes and bought tickets for the next day. Six of them.

At Malaprop's that night, readers asked if we'd get to visit Biltmore while we were in town. I explained that we'd been hesitant to buy them, but we had our tickets in hand. They emphatically told me, again and again, that it was well worth it and we wouldn't regret it.

They were right. The kids were wowed by the house, which was on a scale they'd never experienced before, and enjoyed exploring the grounds. As a bonus, the house was already decorated for Christmas. An audio tour of the estate helped us better understand what we were seeing, and how this was not just a home but a part of history. Looking out on the fall foliage of Biltmore Forest was my favorite part. Having seen it for ourselves, we could appreciate why many considered it the region's must-see attraction.

Signature experiences are often expensive, sometimes achingly so. But Will reminded me that my only Biltmore regret was that we didn't have more time to spend there.

Will built his case, recalling other times we'd (judiciously) spent beyond our comfort zone and were happy to do so even though it felt out of character: a day at Wrigley Field, a trip to the top of the Empire State Building, tickets for *Hamilton*. There was no inexpensive way to do these things, but the expense was worth it every time. We had the memories to prove it. "Don't you think this dinner qualifies as a signature experience?" he asked.

I saw his point. Instead of embracing the good things this experience had to offer, I'd been trying to think my way out of it. But if I could learn to change the calculus—and to focus on what my splurge was really getting me—I could save myself a lot of angst.

Change the Calculus to Decide If a Splurge Is Worth It

Many people struggle with overthinking decisions involving money. Could it be because we struggle to establish a clear way to think about atypical expenditures?

When I'm considering a splurge, I'm often afraid of doing something I'll regret. Not because I can't afford it or don't wish to spend money, but because it's out of character. But as Will pointed out, I'll also regret not doing something that brings me joy just because it costs more than I'm accustomed to paying. Maybe according to our usual calculations it doesn't make sense to spend freely on a fleeting experience, but splurges are unusual situations. How can we think about them in a way that acknowledges their uniqueness?

When I think back on past splurges, I remember them not in terms of cost per minute but in terms of memories—and those indelible moments take up ample space in my mind. My kids still talk about Biltmore, and the Cubs. When we go to the theater, we don't hang on to the program—but the memories last. Of course we could have chosen to forgo those experiences in favor of something cheaper, but when I look at it from this point of view, I'm glad we didn't.

When I think about what I hope to take away from these out-of-the-ordinary experiences, I think about a friend who once told me his favorite childhood memories all begin with the same words: *let's splurge*. His mom loved to splurge, and whenever she said those words, the whole family knew an unforgettable experience was on the horizon.

When Thomas Gilovich and Amit Kumar studied whether people get more happiness from spending money on material goods or spending money on experiences, experiences was the runaway winner. This is largely thanks to the fact that our experiences connect us to others more than material goods do and play a bigger role in our sense of self. "In a very real way, we are the sum total of our experiences," Gilovich and Kumar write.

Even long after they're gone, experiences become memories we treasure and continue to share with others. "We consume experiences directly with other people," says Gilovich. "And after they're gone, they're part of the stories that we tell to one another."

The next time you're considering a splurge, ask yourself, *What is that money really buying me? What do I hope to get out of this experience? How do I measure the return on my investment?* Life is a series of experiences. Our splurges may not come cheap, but the memories are priceless.

Remember That Money Is Not the Only Currency

Thankfully, not all splurges require big bucks. Sometimes a small expenditure feels pleasantly—incredibly—extravagant. One of my kids' favorite memories is from their first trip to New York, when Will and I let them choose whatever they wanted for dinner for our last night in town.

They opted for a cafeteria-style place, the kind where you walk up to the counter, point to what you want, and get it on a plate, immediately. They chose pizza slices that were most definitely not on any "Best of New York" list. And then, the splurge: we let them pick out any drink they wanted from the refrigerated case. At our house, we drink all water, all the time. Soda is way out of character for us, but of course, my kids love it. The drinks cost us a grand total of $8, but money isn't the only currency. My kids appreciated the rare indulgence and talked about their "amazing" dinner for ages.

Sometimes the "spending" is not of dollars but of something else.

My cousin's family lives in a tiny town on the West Coast. My cousin and I were close growing up, and I don't get to see her and her family nearly enough these days—especially since it takes three airplanes to get from our city to theirs. We were over the moon when they announced plans to come stay with us for a week-long visit.

Their last night in town, we planned to stay in. Friday night is our regular pizza night, so we ordered in, early, to accommodate a visiting toddler's schedule. As I cleaned up after dinner, I grabbed my phone for a quick email check; we'd been out and about all day and I wanted to make sure I didn't have any fires to put out before the weekend. Work looked to be in good shape, but another message caught my eye.

For over a year, Will and I had been waiting for a new business to open in our old neighborhood: a combo coffee shop and Popsicle stand that the whole family couldn't wait to patronize, albeit for different reasons. The construction permits hadn't come through as planned, resulting in delay after delay. But now, right there in my email, was the news: they were opening that night for the first time. Just for a few hours, to friends and family only. And Popsicles were free for all.

The kitchen clock read 8:15. We could afford free Popsicles, but could we afford to keep everyone up so late? It was a little past my youngest child's bedtime and well past when my cousin's three-year-old should have been asleep. If we left the house then, *everyone* would be up too late. But the next day my cousin and her family would fly back to California. I was missing them before they'd even left, and besides—wouldn't the time change mess with their body clocks anyway? One last late night wouldn't be the end of us.

I quietly asked my cousin, "Are you up for a dessert run?" Surprised by the question, she looked first at the clock and then her daughter and said, "Why not?" She whispered to her husband, who shrugged, saying, "It's the last night. Let's go." We piled everyone into our minivan and drove to the new Popsicle store.

The place was packed with happy customers, but because nobody had to pay, the line went fast. The real holdup was deciding which flavor to try: passion fruit, strawberry lemonade, or cookies and cream? We lucked into a too-small booth and piled in, enjoying our free Popsicles. The owner made the rounds, asking how we liked our treats and urging us to try another flavor—or even two. "Go back as many times as you want," he said, so we made a return trip to the counter. My teenage son thought he'd died and gone to heaven. We laughed, attempting to try all the flavors by sharing bites across the table. We went to bed too late, way outside our usual routine.

It is my favorite memory from that week.

To New Experiences

Now when I'm deciding whether to splurge, it's all about the experience. And when it came to the kids and our fancy dinner out, I was hoping for unforgettable.

Will said, "Even if it's not the best dinner they've ever had, don't you think they'll *remember* it?"

Of course they would. I was sure of it. And that allowed my frazzled brain to relax.

A few weeks after I panicked about the confirmation email, we packed our bags and headed to Chicago. On our final night in town, we dressed up and went to the restaurant. We coached the kids in advance. "The goal isn't necessarily to enjoy everything," we told them, "but to notice what's interesting. Don't expect it to be the best food you've ever eaten, but notice what's memorable. Pay attention to not just how it tastes, but also how it looks and smells and sounds."

And because kids will be kids, we added, "And no potty jokes."

I was skittish about taking them, but when we walked through the door, the host's eyes lit up immediately upon seeing someone, *anyone*, younger than thirty. We sat down at a table set with a chilled silver bowl at its center—the kind my grandmother used to have—piled high with oranges, rosemary, and other herbs I couldn't identify. (An hour later, a server would carefully pour hot water straight into the centerpiece, sending aromatic steam billowing into the air around us.)

They poured champagne for the adults and procured sparkling apple cider for the kids—in grown-up flutes, of course. Will raised his glass in a toast: "To new experiences," he said, and we all clinked glasses.

For the next three hours, we ate incredible food, unlike—and this is no exaggeration—anything we'd ever had before. Our servers, who were every bit as excited to see our kids as the host was, carefully explained each course, which often required directions on how to eat it.

Two hours into our meal, our servers visited our table and said, "Set your forks down; it's time to take a field trip."

"Did you and Dad do this last time?" our kids asked.

We hadn't. Will and I were grinning like fools, because this was new to us as well. We folded our napkins and followed our servers as we wound our way through the restaurant, finally arriving in the kitchen. *The kitchen!* We took it all in, trying not to gawk at the chefs hard at work all around us, and then the bartender showed us how to make our own cocktails in beautiful, old-fashioned shakers, right there in the renowned kitchen. Gin for the grown-ups, root beer for the kids, delight all around.

We left tired, full, and happy. Before we drove away, we captured a terribly lit photograph on a side street. That's all we have to show for our evening—that and a keepsake menu conceptualized by flavor profiles that makes very little sense when I look at it now.

That dinner was worth every nickel.

·············· Next Steps ··············

1. Do you typically embrace splurging or find that you, too, cringe at the thought of uncharacteristic expenditures?

....

....

....

....

....

....

2. Can you recall a memorable splurge? What was it?

....

....

....

....

....

....

3. Are you reluctant to part with resources other than money—like time, energy, or routine? For what memorable splurge could you try involving one of those things?

....

....

....

....

4. Have you been dreaming about indulging in a special experience? How can you make it happen?

....

....

....

....

13

Small Shifts toward Simple Abundance

"I don't feel very much like Pooh today," said Pooh. "There, there," said Piglet. "I'll bring you tea and honey until you do."

A. A. Milne

I walk into Trader Joe's, list in hand, and immediately encounter the fresh flower display. This is easily my favorite part of the store—well, this and the cheese section—and I'm eager as always to see what's available. I survey the day's options: tulips in a range of pastels, spray roses and long-stem lilies, three different kinds of hydrangeas. *Should I or shouldn't I?* Of course I *want* to, but do I really *need* fresh flowers today?

I debate my options, then finally add hydrangeas to my cart. But maybe I should have gotten tulips? I swap the hydrangeas for lavender tulips and choose some greenery to complete the arrangement. But do I really need it? I am clearly thinking about this too hard. No to the greenery; I can cut that from my own backyard. I put the greenery back. I circle the store, ticking off the items on my list, being careful not to crush the tulips. Do I really need the tulips? I get in line to check out, still looking at the tulips. Maybe I don't really need flowers. If I'm not sure, I should put them back. I take them back to their buckets, then get back in the checkout line.

I pay, load my groceries into my car, then drive home. When I unpack my bags, I realize two things.

I forgot the salad mix I really needed, even though it was right there on my list.

And now that I'm home, surveying my clean but slightly bare countertops, I can see I chose poorly—*I should have bought the flowers.* Even though my groceries are purchased and put away, I'm still spinning my wheels about those flowers.

This decision—and so many like it—is of little consequence. It's about a grocery run, a five-dollar purchase, a grace note for the kitchen counter. This one decision is hardly life-changing.

But then again, life is made up of moments like these. I waste precious minutes debating the inconsequential, talking myself out of things I know will bring me joy, things it wouldn't hurt to say yes to, because though the cost is low, the pleasure is great.

And that's not all. Instead of thinking about the task at hand, I was stuck in my unhelpful thought loop while my attention should have been elsewhere. Say, on the salad mix.

This kind of overthinking is a lose-lose proposition.

A Lose-Lose Proposition

I wish I could tell you my Trader Joe's flower experience was a onetime thing, but that would be a lie. It's the kind of thing I used to do habitually and still catch myself doing from time to time. My inner critic—who isn't as vocal as she used to be, thank goodness—still tries to raise her voice and say, *Is this best? Is this wise? Are you sure you want to do this?* This strict inner policing is something with which many people—especially women—continue to struggle. To overcome these kinds of thoughts, we need to evaluate why they're so easy to fall victim to.

We know overthinking pulls our thoughts in unhelpful directions, as we pursue threads of worry, remorse, or regret. But we may not realize that overthinking also prevents us from welcoming good things into our lives. We cut ourselves off from life's small pleasures, talking ourselves out of potentially good things and wasting a lot of mental energy in the process.

We suspect we'll regret denying ourselves, yet we do it anyway. In one of her most popular newspaper columns, Erma Bombeck wrote that if she had her life to live over, she would "have eaten popcorn in the 'good' living room" and "have burnt the pink candle that was sculptured like a rose before it melted in storage." She wrote those words in 1979, yet the piece continues to circulate and still resonates with women. We see ourselves in those words because we, too, want to enjoy the good things in life while we have the chance. And yet so many of us don't.

When we stop overthinking, we can get out of our own way and bring more joy, peace, and love into our lives. Let's take a look at some things you can do to invite good things into your life instead of overthinking your way out of them.

Resolve to Be Kind to Yourself

What was I trying to get out of those flowers, anyway? I didn't need them; they were a grace note, not an essential. I was fully capable of getting by without them. Those flowers were nice because they were "extra," yet *extra* is something I often talk myself out of.

What I tend to overlook is that buying flowers isn't a frivolous, throwaway expenditure. They may not be strictly necessary, per se, but they do make a big difference in how I think and feel. Once I get them home, it makes me happy to see them on the kitchen counter all week long; it's a little thing that has an outsized effect on my days. And it's so easy to do.

Yet I often deny myself these little things, giving in to the inner critic who questions my small indulgences, precisely because they're *extra*. Or I used to, until I learned to be kinder to myself and got a little more comfortable with the posture of abundance. When I say *abundance*, I don't mean splurging on luxury goods or spending extravagantly on a regular basis. I'm talking about the little things we *enjoy* but don't necessarily *need*.

Too many women confess to being experts at policing their own small treats, holding constant conversations with them-selves. *Should I do that? Is it really worth it?* If we can't bring ourselves to tell our inner critic *yes* (and also to please leave us alone), we'll default to the status quo, which means we miss out on little bursts of happiness. Why do we do this to ourselves? When I blogged about this on *Modern Mrs Darcy*, readers told me they, too, struggled with indulging in small treats. Some con-fessed they had whole drawers full of good things—fine choco-late, French lotion, scented candles—that they'd been given but felt they shouldn't use until a "special" occasion. Whatever the reason, we postpone or altogether skip small treats that bring us joy.

Sometimes we even feel guilty enjoying things we're required to do. I have a friend whose job mandates she spend time reading and researching, two things she delights in. But she once told me this makes her feel guilty. *Aren't you supposed to be working?* her inner critic asks. *Should you really be enjoying this?*

For goodness' sake, she was doing her actual job and doing it well—and still overthinking it!

It doesn't have to be this way. We can learn to treat ourselves gently, and with kindness. We can go from closely monitoring the efficiency of our every move to giving ourselves the grace to not be so darn efficient all the time, from having to continually justify our decisions to feeling released from needing to get everything perfect. We can give ourselves permission to enjoy something that exceeds the minimum we need to get by. We can appreciate the good things right in front of us without feeling guilty about them. We can trade a scarcity mentality for an attitude of abundance.

There was nothing magical about my Trader Joe's bouquet; the point isn't the flowers but what they represent. Sure, we could get by without life's small pleasures, and if we're operating under a scarcity mentality, we do exactly that. But with a posture of abundance, we feel empowered to say yes to this small kindness.

These little decisions seem small, and in a way, they are. But the implications are large: one, we wouldn't mind bringing a little more simple joy into our lives; and two, if we can't trust ourselves to make the right decision about a four-dollar bouquet, it's no wonder we're slow to trust ourselves with the big stuff.

With that in mind, what small things bring you joy? How can you enjoy them on a more regular basis?

Identify Your Small Treats

Iris Murdoch writes, "One of the secrets of a happy life is continuous small treats, and if some of these can be inexpensive and quickly procured so much the better." Murdoch wrote this as a bit of a joke, a line for one of her characters, yet don't we all love small treats?

We can define a "treat" as something extra, something inessential, something that goes beyond the absolute minimum we require. Treats don't have to be expensive, but they should be highly individual and bring *us* joy, regardless of others' tastes and preferences.

When I asked friends what small treats they enjoyed, the responses were varied: a lavender bath on a Tuesday night while somebody else put the kids to bed, a square of good dark chocolate after dinner, a regular Saturday morning hike during the time they used to devote to chores, the anticipation of intriguing new books arriving in the mail on release day.

As for me, after years of using cheap ones, I now indulge in good pens—ones that cost a dollar more than the just-getting-by models. For the longest time, I debated whether spending the extra buck was "worth it." I don't do that anymore, because I'm no longer interested in the bare minimum—at least not when it comes to pens, which matter to me. Sure, I *could* do my writing with a twenty-cent pen—or worse, a free one from the bank—but if I'll enjoy the experience more by paying extra for a good one, I'll opt for the good one every time. Writing with a quality pen is a delight, and paying a little more for a tool that will write for hours and hours is one of the cheapest delights I know.

I have a friend who loves guacamole, and she told me how she used to habitually turn down the guacamole at her favorite taco spot because she didn't need it. But on her last visit, she was in an abundant frame of mind and paid the extra dollar for guacamole. She said it was so good it made her wonder why she'd never ordered it before. We both knew the answer: it wasn't essential, so she'd defaulted to *no*. But she's not going to do that anymore, because she's learning to make the good stuff a habit.

Make the Good Stuff a Habit

One of the most effective ways to bring good things into our lives is to make a habit of it.

Earlier in this book, we discussed how we can put recurring decisions on autopilot, deciding once and enjoying the benefits indefinitely. We can act, like clockwork, for our own benefit without having to endlessly debate whether it's the "right" thing to do. This frees us to enjoy the thing, whatever it is, instead of torturing ourselves about whether we should or shouldn't, or waiting for a special occasion that may never arrive.

When we don't have these decisions settled in our minds in advance, we rely on winging it, making decisions based on how we feel in the moment. We may ask ourselves, *How big of a deal can it be to decide about flowers once we're at the store?* It may not sound hard, but then in the moment, there in the store, we freeze. Without a clear philosophy or system to guide us, we have to continually make decisions and justify them to ourselves.

I put this strategy into action and made a personal rule for myself, specifically about flowers: I will buy flowers every time I'm at Trader Joe's, unless the selection is truly tragic or my own peonies are blooming. Because of that inner maximizer I told you about, plus my innate frugal nature, this wasn't the most natural decision. That's why I chose to put the decision on autopilot; otherwise, I'd wear myself out debating every time I went to the store. Now I just plop them into my cart, no decision required. It costs less than five dollars (although the daffodils I bought this morning were just a dollar fifty), and it makes me really, really happy.

Other people live out this strategy in ways that suit their predilections. When I was in college, I babysat regularly for a nearby family and was fascinated by the way the mom kept the kitchen in order. Tracy wasn't terribly domestic, as she put it, but she did love to cook and called her kitchen her "happy place." When I would arrive at her home after my morning classes, the kids had usually just gone down for their naps, and I'd walk in while she was tidying up her kitchen. She always finished by wiping down the island, then choosing a giant jar candle from her stash under the sink and lighting it. The flickering candle made the kitchen feel snug and welcoming, something I appreciated during the dreary Chicago winters.

Once I sat on a stool at the island, chatting with her as she went through her routine. "I love those candles," I told her as she struck a match. "I'm glad," she said, and then she told me she used to feel bad about lighting them. They were nice candles, and she used to think she should wait for a special occasion to burn them. I asked her what had changed.

"I got over it," she said. "I decided I'd just light them anyway. I really like them, you know? They make me weirdly happy, considering how small a thing a candle is. So I decided I'd light them, all the time."

I'm glad Tracy was able to embrace an abundance mindset and overcome her impulse to save the candles for "special" occasions.

Look for Ways to Add Joy to Your Days

Simple abundance is a frame of mind, not something you can buy; that feeling of plenty doesn't even have to carry a price tag. It can be a time-out during the day to read a novel, or sit and relax on the porch with a cup of tea, or stop to notice your neighbor's flowers. What a gift it is to give ourselves permission to enjoy these little moments.

One place I've learned to practice an abundance mindset is out on the road, when I'm behind the wheel.

To illustrate, here's a story. Once upon a time, I lived in the Chicago suburbs. Will and I thought long and hard about settling down in the Windy City after we got married.

We didn't. The cost of living and the brutal Chicago winters nudged us south, but a crucial third factor in my pro/con list was Roosevelt Road—a wide, strip mall–lined artery through

Chicago's western suburbs that I navigated regularly and hated with the fire of a thousand suns. Or, perhaps, the fire of a thousand exhaust-spewing engines. I resented every minute I spent on that road, even if it was the fastest way to reach my destination.

We ended up back in Louisville, where one particular road reminds me more and more of that dreaded Chicago thoroughfare with every passing year. (For the locals: Shelbyville Road. *Cringe.*)

I drove that road almost daily for years, until one day, undone by the weight of the burgeoning cell phone stores, car dealerships, vast concrete parking lots, stoplights, and yet another Walgreens, I had a revelation: I could take the long way home. I stopped driving the soul-sucking road that day. It's been five years, and I haven't looked back.

I used to overthink whether driving a little bit out of my way to find a more emotionally pleasant route was "worth it." Not anymore. I decided once, and I live by that decision every time I get in the car. Unless my destination is actually on that horrible road—which would make traveling it essential—I don't drive on it. Time and gas are valuable resources, but so are my mental energy, my (generally) chipper attitude, and my patience with endless concrete landscapes. When time is short, I go the fast way, even if it's ugly. But if I have the three minutes to spare, I no longer feel bad about choosing the long way, because traveling a short distance—sometimes just three blocks!—out of my way to prioritize beauty over speed is a small change that makes me much happier.

From Lose-Lose to Win-Win

The point of these small shifts is peace and joy. Overthinking here is lose-lose, but we are doubly enriched if we can put the practice aside and stop thinking ourselves out of happiness.

··········· Next Steps ···········

1. What are some examples of simple abundance in your life?

....

....

....

....

....

2. When it comes to simple pleasures, do you ever catch yourself thinking, *I don't deserve this*? How can you change that inner dialogue?

....

....

....

....

....

14

The Ripple Effect

I change myself, I change the world.

Gloria Anzaldúa

In this book, I've sought to convince you that what you think about matters. By changing your thought life, you can fundamentally change the way you experience the world. What you do with your minutes and hours adds up to a life. My hope is that this book equips you to spend more of those minutes pursuing healthy, helpful, and life-giving thoughts that spur you to take actions that are the same.

How we think—that is, what we think about, what those thoughts mean to us, and what we choose to do about them— determines, to a considerable extent, what our lives are like. As Ralph Waldo Emerson writes, "What is life but what a man is thinking of all day?" We are cultivating the person we are and will become, one thought at a time.

We all want lives that could be described as well-lived. But when we spend our time overthinking, *that* is what we're doing with our life. Overthinking is not just a nuisance; every minute we spend overthinking is a minute not spent on the things that matter.

When I discuss overthinking with other women, so many of them hate that they do it and say they would like to stop. At the same time, they may not consider it a pressing issue. But I fear they underestimate overthinking's effect on their lives—on all our lives. While we tend to think of overthinking as a personal problem, the truth is that our individual thoughts, decisions, and actions don't affect only us; they create a ripple effect that impacts the people around us and carries far and wide.

One of my favorite writers is my fellow Kentuckian Wendell Berry, who has written extensively about the ecological health of our world and our duty to tend it with care. "Small destructions add up," he writes, "and finally they are understood collectively as large destructions." Berry is speaking of the health of our mountains and oceans, but I've come to understand that overthinking has a similar effect on our lives. At best, overthinking is a waste of effort and energy. At worst, it wreaks havoc on our thought lives. Overthinking does no one good and does many of us active harm. These small destructions add up, and not just in our own individual lives. The cumulative toll for all this overthinking is vast.

What if instead of wasting our time overthinking, we focused on the good we might do? Small destructions add up—but so do acts of renewal. What if we sought out these small acts of reclamation? How great might the ripple effect be for our families, our communities, our world?

We Are Continually Creating the World We Live In

At my church, we regularly sing a song in which the chorus repeats, "God will delight when we are creators / of justice and joy, compassion and peace." The first time I heard it, I was captivated by the idea that we don't have to settle for merely *yearning* for these things; we can also *create* them.

We can create justice in our small daily interactions. We can create love and joy, right where we are. We can practice compassion and embody and experience peace. We can create all these good things right in our own lives that affect those around us, who in turn affect their communities, who go on to impact our whole world.

We can be creators of justice, love, joy, compassion, and peace. But when we take a look at the world around us, it's clear these things don't just happen; we have to *think* about them—and then *act* on those thoughts. We need to ask ourselves important questions, such as *What kind of person do I want to be? What kind of world do I want to live in? How can I—in my own small way—make that happen?*

I'm reminded of a time Will and I went to Costco together, which hardly ever happens. We'd just pulled our freshly packed minivan out of the parking lot when we hit a red light. Right there on the corner, a woman held a cardboard sign that read "Homeless, hungry, anything helps."

I had always played these kinds of situations by ear, but I knew I had cash, so I rolled down the window, handed her five bucks, and told her to take care. The light turned green. We traveled in silence for a few blocks, then Will flipped on his blinker to merge. When he glanced over to check his blind spot, his gaze landed on the two hundred or so granola bars we'd just stacked on the middle seat. I could see his shoulders fall.

"We have two hundred granola bars in this car," he said. "We should have given her one. We could have given her a hundred. What were we thinking?"

The thing was, we hadn't thought of it at all. So on that day, we made a new rule for ourselves: if someone who is hungry or homeless asks for our help, we give five dollars and a granola bar. We usually have a little cash on hand, and we keep plenty of snacks in the glove compartment for hungry kids.

A good while after our Costco trip, my family was driving south to the Florida Panhandle for vacation. At a friend's suggestion, we stopped en route at an Alabama fruit stand and bought twenty pounds of ripe peaches. Our car was jam-packed with everything six people would need for a ten-day trip, so there was no place to put them. Will and I nestled the peaches into the console between the driver and passenger seats, propped high on a bunch of odds and ends. I was in the passenger seat and had to steady the heavy box when we went around tight corners.

When we pulled off the highway in Montgomery, a man was on the corner in the midday sun, holding a sign that said "Homeless, hungry." So we did what we do: we rolled down the window to give him five dollars and a granola bar. He said, "God bless," and we said, "Take care." He turned to go and then stopped as though he'd just noticed something. "Can I have one of those?" he asked.

Will was confused and asked, "One of what?"

The man gestured toward the peaches.

"Of course!" we said, and Will handed him a juicy peach off the top.

"Bless you, brother," he said. "I haven't had one of these in so long."

As we drove away, I wondered if we should have handed him the whole container. The answer is, *I don't know.* But I *do* know I'm continually grateful we established that baseline for ourselves, and we have the freedom to deviate from it when necessary— though we surely do so imperfectly.

Is it possible we give money to people who don't use it wisely? Yes. Do I care? No. I decided a long time ago that I want to be generous. I want to live in a world where we help one another; it's not up to me what people do with the money or other resources I give them. And so I don't overthink these questions in the moment, even if I'm still living my way into the answers. I act.

With each action you and I take, we vote for the kind of people we want to be and the kind of world we want to live in. This is what I choose.

The world is big; we are small. The feeling that we can't make a difference can be paralyzing. There's so much to be done. How could what we do possibly matter? It's easy to feel hopeless and helpless, but we don't have to be responsible for complicated solutions. We can begin where we are. We can make a difference. We can be a force for good, for our own sakes and for the world's.

A Benediction

I attend an Episcopal church where, at the close of each service, the priest sends us on our way with a benediction—a "good word" to take with us as we head out into the world. Years ago—and, coincidentally, on my birthday—my priest spoke a benediction so lovely I later asked for a written copy. It captured my hopes not only for the one year ahead but for *all* the years to come. It's about the way we see the world, the thoughts we choose to nurture, and the benefits that result.

I share it with you now:

> May you be peaceful, happy, and light in body and spirit. May you live in safety. May you be free from anxiety and worry. May you learn to look at yourself with the eyes of understanding and love. May you be able to recognize and touch the seeds of joy and happiness in yourself. May you know how to nourish the seeds of joy in yourself every day. May you be able to live fresh, solid, and free.

This says so much about what I want for myself—and what I want for you, dear reader. May you put the strategies in this book to good use. May you put overthinking aside and cultivate a thought life that brings you peace and joy. May you be good to yourself and a force for good in the world.

May *you* be able to live fresh, solid, and free.

Acknowledgments

With every book I write, the list of people to thank gets a little longer. This is as it should be. When I first fell in love with books and reading as a child, I imagined the finished product I held in my hands was the product of an author slaving away at her desk, alone. I know better now. You wouldn't be holding *this* book if countless people hadn't helped me in ways you can't even imagine and I don't want to confess to.

To Rebekah Guzman and Bill Jensen, for the early brainstorming, excellent tidepooling, and support as I struggled to bring this concept to fruition.

To Liz Heaney, working with you again was a pleasure. Thanks for your wise insights and tough but kind criticism, and for not giving up until we found the right structure. You *know* how I feel about structure!

To the great team at Baker Books: Wendy Wetzel and Mark Rice, for your marketing savvy; Brianna DeWitt, for your smart publicity; Amy Ballor, for your copyediting eagle eye; Patti Brinks, for nailing this gorgeous cover on the first try; Brian Thomasson, for your early enthusiasm and for that great story about your mom; and everyone else who makes the publishing magic happen.

Marybeth Whalen, for your boundless enthusiasm for the subject of this book and uncanny ability to text exactly the right words at exactly the right time.

Ally Fallon, for helping me put this thing together from the beginning and for telling me about Thailand.

Ariel Lawhon and J. T. Ellison, whose excellent Scrivener tips dramatically improved my workflow, for providing writerly encouragement right when I need it.

Lisa Patton, for your hospitality that helped get this book written—and also for the salad dressing recommendation.

Melissa Klassen, for being the kind of friend to whom I can entrust a truly terrible first draft, for keeping my life from falling to pieces while I'm on deadline, and for listening to me talk about this thing way too much for way too long. To Randi Thornhill, for being trustworthy with my worst stuff, for providing critical early feedback, and for swapping perfectionism stories with me.

Brenna Frederick and Leigh Kramer, for your careful reading and wise feedback. Donna Hetchler, for your close eyes and countless spreadsheets. Ginger, for making the work we do together *work*. I'm so grateful for you and your (self-professed) complete lack of chill.

Beth Silvers, for pulling me out of many an overthinking circle and for helping me think through many of the ideas that appear in these pages.

Sarah Bessey, for letting me pull the perfect line from your *Field Notes* newsletter to introduce chapter 5.

Sarah Stewart Holland, Kendra Adachi, Jamie B. Golden, Patti Callahan Henry, Mary Laura Philpott, Laura Tremaine, and Erik Fisher for graciously providing words of endorsement for this book.

The problem with befriending writers is you just might end up in the pages of their books. A whole lot of friends ended up in these pages. Huge thanks to Lori Halton, Dave and Amanda Harrity, Ashley Gutierrez Siler, Janssen Bradshaw, Meg Tietz, Myquillyn Smith, and Knox McCoy for their friendship, and for letting me tell their stories.

To the readers of *Modern Mrs Darcy*, for responding with enthusiasm when I floated these ideas out over the years, for serving as a thoughtful and engaged sounding board, and for convincing me that small actions taken with great love change the world.

To the booksellers who stock—and even better, hand-sell!—my books, host me for events, and tell their customers to listen to my podcasts. Thanks for spreading the book love.

To the women of More Jane Eyre: Claire Diaz-Ortiz, Ally Fallon (again), Emily Freeman, Mel Joulwan, and Claire Pelletreau, for serving as a safe sounding board, for cheering me on and calling me out, and for doing so with grace, wisdom, and compassion.

Laura Vanderkam, Chris Bailey, Camille Noe Pagán, and Katherine Chen, for the shoptalk and for being generous with your knowledge about the writing life.

Mom and Dad, I can't seem to talk about what I've learned in life without talking about you. I'm sorry you're the subject of so many of my early examples. Thanks for graciously allowing me to use them.

To Jackson, Sarah, Lucy, and Silas, for teaching me so much about this topic and everything else that's worth knowing, for letting me (obliquely) tell your stories, and for putting up with me leaving my pages all over the kitchen counter. You guys are the greatest.

To Will, for everything. Now let's enjoy some time together *not* on deadline.

Notes

Chapter 1 How We Spend Our Lives

15 **Her studies over a twenty-year period:** Dr. Susan Nolen-Hoeksema, *Women Who Think Too Much: How to Break Free of Overthinking and Reclaim Your Life* (New York: Henry Holt, 2003), 16.

15 **Annie Dillard writes:** Annie Dillard, *The Writing Life*, in *Three by Annie Dillard: Pilgrim at Tinker Creek, An American Childhood, The Writing Life* (New York: HarperCollins, 1990), 568.

16 **We are suffering from an epidemic:** Nolen-Hoeksema, *Women Who Think Too Much*, 3.

16 **Researchers at the Amen Clinics:** "Women Have More Active Brains than Men," ScienceDaily, August 7, 2017, https://www.science daily.com/releases/2017/08/170807120521.htm.

16 **Women can ruminate:** Nolen-Hoeksema, *Women Who Think Too Much*, 5.

17 **One study analyzing birth cohort differences:** Thomas Curran and Andrew P. Hill, "Perfectionism Is Increasing Over Time: A Meta-analysis of Birth Cohort Differences from 1989 to 2016," *Psychological Bulletin* 145, no. 4 (April 2019), 410–29.

Chapter 2 Work the Process

30 **Since childhood we have spent:** Dr. Henry Emmons, *The Chemistry of Calm: A Powerful, Drug-Free Plan to Quiet Your Fears and Overcome Your Anxiety* (New York: Touchstone, 2010), 157.

30 **Many of us strengthen:** Emmons, *Chemistry of Calm*, 235.

31 **Doing something small:** Nolen-Hoeksema, Women Who Think Too Much, 93.

32 **If we can stop reinforcing:** Emmons, *Chemistry of Calm*, 234–35.

Chapter 5 Take Time to Make Time

69 **To get my literal house in order:** The phrase "complete the cycle" is in common usage, but I first encountered it in Shifrah Combiths, "Try the 'Complete the Cycle' Cleaning Method for Instant Results," Apartment Therapy, accessed July 29, 2019, https://www.apartmenttherapy.com/try-complete-the-cycle-and-see-how-much-less-you-have-to-pick-up-221322.

69 *A Modern Mrs Darcy* **blog reader:** This conversation unfolded in the blog comments of a post I wrote called "Completing the Cycle," published March 6, 2017, on *Modern Mrs Darcy* and available at: https://modernmrsdarcy.com/completing-the-cycle.

72 **From a dystopian literary novel:** The book that held the "clean left to right" advice is Louise Erdrich's novel *Future Home of the Living God* (New York: HarperCollins, 2017). While this absolutely wasn't the point of the story, it stuck with me.

72 **The straightest path to efficiency:** Susan C. Pinsky, *Organizing for People with ADHD* (Beverly, MA: Fair Winds Press, 2012), 23.

73 **The basic housekeeping functions:** Dr. Bessel van der Kolk, *The Body Keeps the Score: Brain, Mind, and Body in the Healing of Trauma* (New York: Penguin, 2014), 56.

73 **The fascinating book:** Though *The Body Keeps the Score* came highly recommended by myriad readers with good taste, I put off reading it for years because I feared it would be hard and heavy. (It does have "trauma" in the title, after all.) While Van der Kolk certainly addresses difficult subjects, the main descriptor I'd use is *fascinating*. Once I began reading, I couldn't turn the pages fast enough.

73 **Breathing, eating, sleeping:** Van der Kolk, *Body Keeps*, 56.

74 **If something is bad:** Emmons, *Chemistry of Calm*, 10.

74 **Imagine a drug:** Emmons, *Chemistry of Calm*, 118.

74 **The economics of energy:** Emmons, *Chemistry of Calm*, 101.

75 **Fake breaks:** Laura Vanderkam, "Go Confidently: A Conversation with Laura Vanderkam," hosted by Norton Healthcare, Louisville, Kentucky, March 12, 2018.

75 **On the virtue of "conscious breaks":** Laura Vanderkam, *Off the Clock: Feel Less Busy While Getting More Done* (New York: Portfolio, 2018), 93.

Chapter 6 Speed Up to Move On

89 **The *Smitten Kitchen* recipe:** The recipe for Spaghetti Squash and Black Bean Tacos with Queso Fresco can be found in Deb Perelman, *The Smitten Kitchen Cookbook: Recipes and Wisdom from an Obsessive Home Cook* (New York: Knopf, 2012, 143–44), but if you come over for taco night, I'll make them for you myself.

Chapter 7 Tend Your Garden

95 **Tell me what you eat:** Jean Anthelme Brillat-Savarin, *The Physiology of Taste: Or Meditations on Transcendental Gastronomy*, trans. and ed. M. F. K. Fisher (1949), found in the Everyman's Library Edition (New York: Alfred A. Knopf, 2009), 15. I first stumbled upon this line in the introduction to Mason Currey's *Daily Rituals: How Artists Work* (New York: Alfred A. Knopf, 2016).

95 **Your life is the creation:** Winifred Gallagher, *Rapt: Attention and the Focused Life* (New York: Penguin, 2009), 4.

95 **Particularly nasty:** Gallagher, *Rapt*, 3.

97 **What we feel and think:** Dallas Willard, *Renovation of the Heart: Putting on the Character of Christ* (Colorado Springs, CO: NavPress, 2002), 34.

97 **As you would a private garden:** Gallagher, *Rapt*, 53.

98 **The mind is its own place:** John Milton, *Paradise Lost*, bk. 1, lines 254–55.

98 **Animals classified as ruminants:** Emmons, *Chemistry of Calm*, 45.

98 **These negative thoughts:** Nolen-Hoeksema, *Women Who Think Too Much*, 3.

98 **When we ruminate:** Emmons, *Chemistry of Calm*, 151.

100 **Hard writing:** Wallace Stegner, *Crossing to Safety* (New York: Random House, 1987), 158.

101 **John Gottman:** Dr. John M. Gottman and Nan Silver, *The Seven Principles for Making Marriage Work: A Practical Guide from the Country's Foremost Relationship Expert* (New York: Harmony Books, 1999), 73–74.

101 **To make gratitude a habit:** Zach Brittle, LMHC, "G Is for Gratitude," *The Gottman Relationship Blog*, March 31, 2014, https://www.gottman .com/blog/g-is-for-gratitude.

102 **This exercise in creativity:** Katty Kay and Claire Shipman, *The Confidence Code: The Science and Art of Self-Assurance—What Women Should Know* (New York: HarperCollins, 2014), 149.

103 **What would I tell my best friend?:** Chip Heath and Dan Heath, *Decisive: How to Make Better Choices in Life and Work* (New York: Crown Business, 2013), 172. I love this simple question and now use it all the time. *Decisive* is the first place I encountered it.

103 **What would I like about this?:** "An Interview with Peter Schjeldahl," *Blackbird Archive: An Online Journal of Literature and the Arts* 3, no. 1 (Spring 2004). This question comes from art critic Peter Schjeldahl, who was actually talking about evaluating works of art. But I've found I can rephrase the question to encompass a wide variety of situations, including meetings, conversations, and, especially, literature. The excellent interview from which this question was drawn is found at https://blackbird.vcu.edu/v3n1/gallery/schjeldahl_p/interview_text.htm.

104 **My friend Beth:** Many thanks to Beth Silvers for her wisdom on this and many other topics. You may know Beth from her podcast, *Pantsuit Politics*, or her book, cowritten with Sarah Stewart Holland, *I Think You're Wrong (But I'm Listening): A Guide to Grace-Filled Political Conversations* (Nashville: Thomas Nelson, 2019). I can't tell you how many times I've said, "Everyone should have a Beth in their life."

104 **Anne Lamott writes:** Anne Lamott, *Almost Everything: Notes on Hope* (New York: Riverhead Books, 2018), 21–23.

105 **Has these unwelcome thoughts:** If you experience depressive or suicidal thoughts, please seek professional help right away. The National Suicide Prevention Lifeline is available 24/7 at 1-800-273-8255.

105 **The vast majority:** Dr. Sally M. Winston and Dr. Martin N. Seif, *Overcoming Unwanted Intrusive Thoughts: A CBT-Based Guide to Getting Over Frightening, Obsessive, or Disturbing Thoughts* (Oakland: New Harbinger Publications, Inc., 2017), 7.

105 **The simple truth:** Winston and Seif, *Overcoming Unwanted Intrusive Thoughts*, 14.

105 **Johnny Cash:** Phil Patton, "Our Longing for Lists," *New York Times*, September 1, 2012, https://www.nytimes.com/2012/09/02/opinion/sunday/our-longing-for-lists.html. The article contained an image of Johnny Cash's to-do list, provided by Julien's Auctions Beverly Hills. The list sold at auction on December 5, 2010, for $6,250.

106 **Rather than allowing:** Amy Morin, *13 Things Mentally Strong Women Don't Do: Own Your Power, Channel Your Confidence, and Find Your Authentic Voice for a Life of Meaning and Joy* (New York: HarperCollins, 2019), 109.

106 **Morin calls journaling:** Morin, *13 Things*, 116.

107 **You can take this a step further:** Pablo Briñol, Richard E. Petty, Margarita Gascó Rivas, and Javier Horcajo, "Treating Thoughts as

Material Objects Can Increase or Decrease Their Impact on Evaluation," *Psychological Science* 24, no. 1 (November 2012), 41–47. Interestingly, some studies that have examined this have mused that the power of ritual is one of the reasons why writing negative thoughts down and throwing them away is effective.

107 **Giving people positive distractions:** Nolen-Hoeksema, *Women Who Think Too Much*, 61.

Chapter 8 Limit Yourself to Free Yourself

113 **All about repetition:** Twyla Tharp, *The Creative Habit: Learn It and Use It for Life* (New York: Simon & Schuster, 2003), 15.

114 **A solid routine fosters:** Mason Currey, *Daily Rituals: How Artists Work* (New York: Alfred A. Knopf, 2013), xiv. Ironically, on the same page, Currey notes, "This book's title is *Daily Rituals*, but my focus in writing it was really people's *routines*."

117 **Even former President Obama:** Michael Lewis, "Obama's Way," *Vanity Fair*, September 11, 2012, https://www.vanityfair.com/news/20 12/10/michael-lewis-profile-barack-obama.

118 **The truly well-organized women:** Carrie Donovan, "Feminism's Effect on Fashion," *New York Times*, August 28, 1977, page 225, accessed online at the *New York Times* archives on June 7, 2019, https://www.ny times.com/1977/08/28/archives/feminisms-effect-on-fashion.html.

118 **Develop a uniform:** William Norwich, "At Mortimer's with Carrie Donovan, the Old Navy Lady," *Observer*, January 26, 1998, https://observer .com/1998/01/at-mortimers-with-carrie-donovan-the-old-navy-lady/.

118 **I don't want to think about:** Lesley M. M. Blume, "Grace Coddington Talks Unconventional Beauty, Too-Skinny Models, and Her 'Unpopular' Wardrobe," *Huffington Post: Life*, March 18, 2010, https:// www.huffpost.com/entry/grace-coddington-talks-un_n_329008.

118 **The ten-item wardrobe:** Jennifer L. Scott, *Lessons from Madame Chic: 20 Stylish Secrets I Learned While Living in Paris* (New York: Simon & Schuster, 2011), 41–56.

121 **You now have the opportunity:** Barry Schwartz, *The Paradox of Choice* (New York: HarperCollins, 2005), 30.

Chapter 9 Get Someone Else to Do It

127 **Fellow podcaster Knox McCoy:** If you don't already know Knox McCoy from *The Popcast with Knox & Jamie*, the long-running podcast he cohosts with Jamie B. Golden, please check it out immediately. He's also the author of the excellently titled book *The Wondering*

Years: How Pop Culture Helped Me Answer Life's Biggest Questions
(Nashville: Thomas Nelson, 2018).

130 **My friend Meg:** Please check out Meg Tietz's top-notch women's lifestyle podcast *Sorta Awesome*, available wherever you get your podcasts.

134 **My friend Myquillyn:** For more of Myquillyn's brilliance, I recommend checking out her book *Cozy Minimalist Home: More Style, Less
Stuff* (Grand Rapids: Zondervan, 2018).

Chapter 10 When Things Go Sideways

151 **I'm reminded of a scene:** *Sideways*, directed by Alexander Payne
(Los Angeles: Fox Searchlight Pictures, 2004), DVD.

Chapter 11 Rituals to Rely On

161 **Rituals benefit even those:** Alison Wood Brooks, Juliana Schroeder,
Jane Risen, Francesca Gino, Adam D. Galinsky, Michael I. Norton,
and Maurice Schweitzer, "Don't Stop Believing: Rituals Improve Performance by Decreasing Anxiety," *Organizational Behavior and Human
Decision Processes* 137 (November 2016): 71–85.

164 **Family dinner:** The most comprehensive study on the subject comes
from Sandra L. Hofferth and John F. Sandberg, "Changes in American
Children's Time," 1981–1997, *Advances in Life Course Research* 6 (December 2001): 193–229. Additional research and information, including
more current studies, are collected at https://thefamilydinnerproject.org.

Chapter 12 Let's Splurge

175 **In a very real way:** Thomas Gilovich and Amit Kumar, "We'll Al-
ways Have Paris: The Hedonic Payoff from Experiential and Material
Investments," in *Advances in Experimental Social Psychology*, eds. M.
Zanna and J. Olson, vol. 51 (New York: Elsevier, 2015), 163.

175 **We consume experiences:** Jay Cassano, "The Science of Why You
Should Spend Your Money on Experiences, Not Things," *Fast Company*, March 30, 2015, https://www.fastcompany.com/3043858/the
-science-of-why-you-should-spend-your-money-on-experiences-not
-thing.

Chapter 13 Small Shifts toward Simple Abundance

185 **Erma Bombeck wrote:** Erma Bombeck, *Eat Less Cottage Cheese and
More Ice Cream: Thoughts on Life from Erma Bombeck* (Kansas City:
Andrews McMeel Publishing, 2003).

187 **One of the secrets:** Iris Murdoch, *The Sea, the Sea* (London: Chatto & Windus, 1978), 81.

Chapter 14 The Ripple Effect

193 **What is life:** Ralph Waldo Emerson, *The Complete Works of Ralph Waldo Emerson: Natural History of Intellect, and Other Papers*, vol. 12 (Boston; New York: Houghton, Mifflin, 1903–04), 10.

194 **Small destructions add up:** Wendell Berry, "Contempt for Small Places," *The Way of Ignorance* (Berkeley: Shoemaker & Hoard, 2005), 26. The full passage reads like this: "The health of the oceans depends on the health of rivers; the health of rivers depends on the health of small streams; the health of small streams depends on the health of their watersheds. The health of the water is exactly the same as the health of the land; the health of small places is exactly the same as the health of large places. As we know, disease is hard to confine. Because natural law is in force everywhere, infections move.

"We cannot immunize the continents and the oceans against our contempt for small places and small streams. Small destructions add up, and finally they are understood collectively as large destructions."

194 **God will delight:** Shirley Erena Murray, "For Everyone Born, a Place at the Table" (Carol Stream, IL: Hope Publishing Company, 1998).

197 **May you be peaceful:** Tracking down the source of this benediction wasn't easy. My priest told me it was from Thomas Merton, and a version does indeed appear in Thomas Merton's book *Contemplative Prayer* (New York: Crown Publishing Group, 1996), 13–16. But my priest adapted her benediction from a prayer that Thich Nhat Hanh shared in his introduction to the book. And that prayer is just one expression of an ancient Buddhist prayer practiced by all schools of Buddhism.

For Further Reading

As an avid reader, I thoroughly enjoyed researching the various aspects of overthinking while writing this book. If you're interested in exploring more on these topics, I enthusiastically recommend the following titles:

Daily Rituals: How Artists Work by Mason Currey

The concept of this compendium couldn't be simpler: the daily routines of writers, composers, painters, choreographers, playwrights, poets, philosophers, sculptors, filmmakers, and scientists, those working both today and hundreds of years ago. Read it straight through or peruse each artist's daily rhythms at leisure. This is by no means a how-to manual. The routines and rituals in these pages are confounding and contradictory, and it's impossible not to notice how many artists' lives and careers were wrecked by substance abuse. But this is an excellent book to get you thinking about what the structure of your life could look like. Take inspiration where you find it, and return to its pages again and again when you're feeling stalled or stymied in your work.

The Chemistry of Calm: A Powerful, Drug-Free Plan to Quiet Your Fears and Overcome Your Anxiety by Dr. Henry Emmons

I first discovered this book when a podcast guest recommended it in what quickly became one of my favorite episodes of *What Should I Read Next?* (That's episode 93: "Books to help you manage anxiety + a book brunch that will have you drooling.") The bulk of this book is about building a strong foundation for mental and physical well-being. In detailed chapters, Emmons explores how the right diet, regular exercise, nutritional supplements, and a practice of mindfulness affect the way our bodies operate and feel. He also explores why anxiety affects so many people today, the seven different types of anxiety, and how we can cultivate resilience for our bodies and minds. Each time I return to this book, my biggest takeaway is not to neglect the basics, even when our problems seem far too complicated to be helped by simple things like good food, exercise, and sleep.

The Next Right Thing: A Simple, Soulful Practice for Making Life Decisions by Emily P. Freeman

Freeman writes for the chronically hesitant, the second-guessers, and anyone who struggles with decision fatigue. I love her podcast of the same name, and this beautiful book stands just fine on its own (though I highly recommend listening to at least a few episodes of the podcast so you can hear Emily voice her stories herself). Whether you are in a season of transition or simply trying to smooth the rough edges of your daily routines, Freeman offers sage advice. Her prayers and practices will leave you feeling refreshed and ready for your next step.

Rapt: Attention and the Focused Life by Winifred Gallagher

Gallagher's story begins with a scary diagnosis. Upon learning of her grim prognosis, Gallagher has a realization: while it would be easy for the disease to monopolize her attention during treatment, the quality of her life would largely be determined by what she chose to pay attention to. She is determined to spend her limited mental currency wisely, and instead of focusing on her illness, she chooses to focus on her life—both the small pleasures like walks and movies and the big ones that give life meaning. In this book, she shares what she has learned about the power of attention, how to cultivate it even when it feels difficult, and why it matters.

Decisive: How to Make Better Choices in Life and Work by Chip and Dan Heath

This story-driven business book explores why some decisions are so challenging, then, drawing on case studies on everything from whether to fire an employee to whether to undergo a risky bone marrow transplant, teaches how to make better ones. The Heath brothers are whip-smart and really funny, making *Decisive* a million times better than your typical business book. Everyone will find a useful takeaway, even if they don't struggle mightily with decisions. I use the information I learned from this book nearly every day.

13 Things Mentally Strong People Don't Do: Take Back Your Power, Embrace Change, Face Your Fears, and Train Your Brain for Happiness and Success by Amy Morin

Through Morin's work as a therapist, she has come to believe that people intent on reaching their greatest potential don't engage in counterproductive bad habits. They make progress not just because of what they do but because of what they *don't* do. Her work contains abundant food for thought about your own thought patterns, habits, and routines, plus solid tips on developing and maintaining mental strength. You may also appreciate Morin's female-specific follow-up, *13 Things Mentally Strong Women Don't Do*, in which she examines why habits like perfectionism, overthinking, self-doubt, and deflecting praise are so destructive—and what women can do instead.

The Creative Habit: Learn It and Use It for Life by Twyla Tharp

In this conversational book, world-renowned choreographer Twyla Tharp illustrates how her life revolves around a whole "arsenal of routines" because, as she says, "a dancer's life is all about repetition." Her general philosophy is that creativity is not an attribute some lucky people possess but something we all can cultivate. Her focus is on shaping the skeleton—the day-to-day structure—of a creative life. Creativity is *work*, in her eyes, and those engaged in creative pursuits would be well-served to implement routines and eliminate distractions. Inspiring and surprisingly practical.

Off the Clock: Feel Less Busy While Getting More Done by Laura Vanderkam

Plenty of people get tons done but still feel frustrated with how they're spending their time. Vanderkam examines highly productive people who—despite their commitments, obligations, and successful enterprises—feel like they have all the time in the world, and she investigates what exactly they're doing that causes them to feel that way. Vanderkam presents seven key mindset shifts using stories about real people, which makes this time-management book both helpful and fun to read.

Renovation of the Heart: Putting on the Character of Christ by Dallas Willard

Do you ever feel like everything would change if you could really understand a book? That's how I feel about the writings of the late, great Dallas Willard, the beloved philosophy professor who spent an incredible forty-eight years at the University of Southern California. His books are so meaty that I read them at about a quarter of my normal speed. This specific book—my favorite of his, if I'm forced to choose—is written for Christians and is about carefully cultivating one's inner self to resemble Christ. The specific focus is on the process of spiritual formation: how your body, soul, mind, and spirit come together to make you *you*. It's packed with rich insights that I'm still working to understand even though I've read it at least five times cover to cover.

Overcoming Unwanted Intrusive Thoughts: A CBT-Based Guide to Getting Over Frightening, Obsessive, or Disturbing Thoughts by Dr. Sally M. Winston and Dr. Martin N. Seif

The title says it all, right? This one is worthy of "best book you've never heard of" status. In this practical guide, Winston and Seif explain how to deal with an uncomfortable truth: our precious attention can be hijacked by junk—and at some point, it will happen to almost all of us. The authors explore what intrusive thoughts are, debunk common myths surrounding these unwelcome thoughts (be they fleeting or persistent), explain strategies to handle them when they happen (something I was doing *very* wrong myself), and illustrate what it looks like to get over them for good.

About the Author

When it comes to approaching her writing and life, Anne Bogel takes a line from Emily Dickinson: "I dwell in possibility." She is adept at viewing old ideas from a fresh perspective and presenting them to the reader in such a way that they experience it as if for the first time.

In 2011, Anne launched her blog, *Modern Mrs Darcy*, which derives its name from Jane Austen. It didn't slot neatly into the existing blog niches (although she's been pleased to hear it described as "a lifestyle blog for nerds"), yet it quickly gained a cult following of smart, thoughtful readers who love Anne's modus operandi of approaching old, familiar ideas from new and fresh angles.

And Anne's readers like to read. While *Modern Mrs Darcy* is not strictly a book blog, Anne writes frequently about books and reading. Her book lists are among her most popular posts. She is well known by readers, authors, and publishers as a tastemaker. In 2016, she launched her podcast *What Should I Read Next?*—a popular show devoted to literary matchmaking, bibliotherapy, and all things books and reading. In 2019, she launched its sister podcast *One Great Book*, where every week Anne pulls one beloved selection off her personal bookshelves and tells listeners all about it in ten minutes or less.

Anne lives in Louisville, Kentucky, with her husband and four children.

MODERN
Mrs Darcy

Connect with Anne through her blog, book club, and podcast (*What Should I Read Next?*) at
ModernMrsDarcy.com.

WHAT SHOULD I READ NEXT?

with anne bogel

Understanding Your
Personality

"This is the book I didn't even know I was waiting for. I can't wait to share it with everyone I know."

—Emily P. Freeman, *Wall Street Journal* bestselling author of *Simply Tuesday* and *The Next Right Thing*

Reflections on the DELIGHTS and DILEMMAS of the Reading Life

Remember the book that first hooked you, the place where you first fell in love with reading, and all the books and moments afterward that helped make you the reader you are today.

LIKE THIS
BOOK?
Consider sharing it with others!

- Share or mention the book on your social media platforms. Use the hashtag **#DontOverthinkIt**.

- Write a book review on your blog or on a retailer site.

- Pick up a copy for friends, family, or anyone who you think would enjoy and be challenged by its message!

- Share this message on Twitter, Facebook, or Instagram:
  I loved #DontOverthinkIt by @AnneBogel // @ReadBakerBooks

- Recommend this book for your church, workplace, book club, or class.

- Follow Baker Books on social media and tell us what you like.

 ReadBakerBooks

 ReadBakerBooks

 ReadBakerBooks